Student Workbook

FOUNDATIONS OF
PERSONAL FINANCE

Teacher's Annotated Workbook

8th Edition

Sally R. Campbell
Winnetka, Illinois

Publisher
The Goodheart-Willcox Company, Inc.
Tinley Park, Illinois
www.g-w.com

Introduction

This *Student Workbook* is designed for use with the text *Foundations of Personal Finance*. It will help you recall and review concepts presented in the text. It will also help you apply what you have learned as you participate in the economic system.

The activities in this guide are divided into chapters that correspond to chapters in the text. After reading the text, do as many exercises in the activity guide as you can without referring to the text. Refer to the text for answers to questions you could not complete and to compare your answers with information in *Foundations of Personal Finance*.

Some of the activities require factual answers. Others ask for opinions, evaluations, and conclusions that cannot be judged as right or wrong. The object of these activities is to encourage you to consider alternatives and evaluate situations thoughtfully. You should be able to defend, explain, and justify your answers and conclusions.

Contents

Unit 3
Managing Your Spending

Unit 4
Planning Your Future

Market or Command?

Activity A	Name ______________________________________
Chapter 1	Date ________________ Period ______________

Place an *M* beside those phrases or terms that describe market economies and a *C* beside those that describe command economies.

C   1. Central authority controls economic activities.

M   2. Consumers choose how to earn and spend money.

M   3. Ideal for starting a business.

M   4. Emphasis on consumer.

C   5. Limited consumer choices.

C   6. Often associated with a socialist or communist form of government.

M   7. Businesses are encouraged to compete with each other.

C   8. Prices of goods set by government or central authority.

M   9. Supply and demand.

M   10. Many product choices are available.

M   11. Often associated with a democratic form of government.

M   12. Innovation sparks growth and prosperity.

C   13. Consumers cannot decide for themselves how to earn and spend income.

C   14. A central authority allocates resources.

C   15. Producers produce what planners recommend.

Compare the major differences between a market and a command economy.

In a command economy, economic decisions are made by a central authority, usually the government. Consumers do not have the right to choose how they earn and spend their money.

A market economy is driven by private ownership and control of productive resources; profit motive; free economic choice; and competition. Consumers' needs and wants control the economy through supply and demand.

Money Makers

Name _______________________________

Date _________________ Period _______________

One of the advantages of a market economy is the freedom of individuals to choose their own way of turning their resources into income or profits. This opportunity exists for all age groups. Using your own ideas, Internet sources, and library references, list and briefly describe five moneymaking ideas that would be possible for a young person to accomplish. Compare and discuss your list with other members of the class.

1. (Student response.)

____

____

____

2. (Student response.)

____

____

____

3. (Student response.)

____

____

____

4. (Student response.)

____

____

____

5. (Student response.)

____

____

____

Local Economy in Action

Name _______________________________

Date ____________________ Period _______________

Arrange an interview with a local merchant to learn how basic economic concepts are applied in the business world. Seek answers to the following questions.

1. Who owns the business? (Student response.) _______________________________

   Who makes most of the decisions on the use of *productive resources*, such as labor, land, and capital?
   (Student response.) _______________________________

   ____

   ____

   ____

2. How do *supply* and *demand* affect the business? (Student response.) _______________________________

   ____

   ____

   ____

3. How does the desire for *profit* influence business decisions and operations? (Student response.) _______________________________

   ____

   ____

   ____

4. How does *competition* influence business decisions and operations? (Student response.) _______________________________

   ____

   ____

   ____

5. What do *free economic choices* mean to the business and its customers? (Student response.) _______________________________

   ____

   ____

   ____

The Basis of a Market Economy

Activity D   Name ______________________________

Chapter 1   Date ________________   Period ____________

Basic characteristics of a market economy are listed below. Examples are given describing each characteristic. In the space provided, write examples of your own to illustrate each.

Basic Characteristics	Example	Your Example
1. Private ownership and control of productive resources	A board of bank directors votes to make loans only to local individuals and businesses.	(Student response.)
2. Supply and demand	Working mothers create a demand for reliable, affordable care for their children. Two teachers open a child care center to meet the demand.	(Student response.)
3. The profit motive	Investors buy stock in a company because the price of the stock is expected to go up and they want to make a profit.	(Student response.)
4. Competition	A hospital loses patients to a new emergency care center that promises immediate emergency care at lower cost.	(Student response.)
5. Free economic choices	Consumers in an area with three supermarkets, a farmer's market, and two convenience stores offer a lot of choices in deciding where to shop for food.	(Student response.)

Chapter 2
Government and the Economy

It's the Law

Activity A
Chapter 2

Name _______________________________________

Date _________________   Period _______________

Select a product that you use frequently. Investigate the regulations that control the product. Briefly describe how these regulations affect the product in each of the following areas.

Product: _______________________________________

1. Manufacturing: (Student response.) _______________________________________

____

____

____

2. Distribution: (Student response.) _______________________________________

____

____

____

3. Advertising: (Student response.) _______________________________________

____

____

____

4. Packaging: (Student response.) _______________________________________

____

____

____

(Continued)

Name_______________________________________

5. Labeling: (Student response.)

____

____

____

6. Sales: (Student response.)

____

____

____

7. Use: (Student response.)

____

____

____

8. Disposal: (Student response.)

____

____

____

9. Price: (Student response.)

____

____

____

10. Other: (Student response.)

____

____

____

Government Agencies Serving You

Name ____

Date __________________ Period _______________

Select one federal, one state, and one local government agency offering services to consumers.
Complete the chart below by finding out the necessary information.

	Federal	State	Local
Name of agency	(Chart answers are student response.)		
Name of agency head			
Address of agency			
Telephone number			
Web site			
Primary purpose and function of the agency			
Services provided			
Eligibility requirements for receiving services			
Procedure for obtaining services			
Number of employees			
Annual budget			

Government Agencies and Their Functions

Name ____

Date _______________________ Period _______________

Identify the government agency indicated by each abbreviation. Then match the agencies to their functions below.

A. CPSC _____Consumer Product Safety Commission._____________________

B. DOL _____Department of Labor_____________________

C. FDA _____Food and Drug Administration._____________________

D. FTC_____Federal Trade Commission._____________________

E. HHS _____Department of Health and Human Services._____________________

F. HUD_____Department of Housing and Urban Development_____________________

G. OSHA _____Occupational Safety and Health Administration._____________________

H. SEC_____Security and Exchange Commission._____________________

I. SSA _____Social Security Administration_____________________

J. USDA_____United States Department of Agriculture._____________________

___A___ 1. Regulates and sets standards for the safety of consumer and children's products.

___I___ 2. Administers the federal government's retirement, survivors and disability insurance, and the supplemental security income programs.

___D___ 3. Responsible for preventing unfair, false, or deceptive advertising, packaging, and selling of consumer products.

___F___ 4. Provides home ownership and rental assistance for low and moderate-income families.

___E___ 5. Promotes public health and works to control drug and alcohol abuse.

___C___ 6. Regulates the manufacturing, labeling, and packaging of foods, drugs, and cosmetics to ensure consumer safety.

___G___ 7. Administers safety and health regulations and standards in the workplace.

___H___ 8. Protects investors against fraud in the buying and selling of securities.

___J___ 9. Regulates the grading and inspection of food.

___B___ 10. Promotes the welfare of wage earners.

"

Chapter 3
Consumers in the Economy: An Overview

Money Talks

Activity A

Chapter 3

Name _______________________________________

Date ________________________ Period _______________

The following quotations are related to spending behavior. Under each quotation, rewrite it in your own words to show that you understand its meaning.

1. *"He who buys what he does not need steals from himself."* Swedish Proverb __(Student response.)____

    ____

    ____

2. *"Spare and have is better than spend and crave."* Ben Franklin _(Student response.)_______

    ____

    ____

3. *"A fool and his money are soon parted."* George Buchanan _(Student response.)________

    ____

    ____

4. *"Economy is too late at the bottom of the purse."* Seneca_(Student response.)__________

    ____

    ____

5. *"He who buys what he does not want will soon want that which he cannot buy."* Anonymous _________

    (Student response.)____

    ____

6. *"Beware of little expenses; a small leak will sink a great ship."* Ben Franklin _(Student response.)___

    ____

    ____

7. In the space below, write your own quotation related to spending behavior. "_______________

    (Student response.)____

    ____ "

Understanding a Market Economy

<table>
<tr><td>Activity B</td><td>Name ______________________________</td></tr>
<tr><td>Chapter 3</td><td>Date ______________   Period ______________</td></tr>
</table>

Respond briefly to the following questions and directions.

1. Explain how earning your way in a market economy relates to your standard of living. _________
   If your income rises faster than prices, more goods and services will be available to you and your standard of living and quality of life will rise. Your earning power and job performance are directly related to your standard of living.

2. Discuss how overall consumer spending impacts the economy at large. When consumers believe the economy is strong or improving, they tend to spend more. This creates a greater demand for goods and services. Businesses expand and create more jobs. This leads to economic prosperity. When consumers are doubtful about the economic future, they spend and borrow less. The demand for goods and services lowers. Businesses slow down because sales decline. Jobs are harder to find and workers are laid off. These conditions can lead to a recession.

3. Give two examples to show how the savings of consumers are pumped back into the economic system to help pay for business growth and expansion. It is loaned to businesses to pay for business growth and building construction. It is loaned to other consumers for the purchases of homes.

4. Discuss the impact of consumer use of credit on individual and family money management and on the economy. The overuse of credit leads to an eventual economic downturn because the credit used today must be repaid with tomorrow's dollars. That means tomorrow's dollars will be paying today's debts rather than supporting future demand. Using credit increases immediate demand, but it decreases future demand.

5. Briefly describe three types of insurance protection. life, health, and property (such as home and automobile)

6. Provide an example to illustrate how consumer investments pay for business growth and activity. Businesses use the money to help purchase new plants and equipment. Investments also help pay for the research and development of new technology and the marketing of new products and services.

7. List at least five examples of public services and facilities people vote for that raise taxes. Include examples from the local, state, and federal levels of government. (List five:) the military, highways, the judicial system, schools, parks, police protection

Consumer Economic Activities

Name _______________________________

Date _______________ Period _______________

Consumer competence offers benefits to the individual and to the economy. In the chart provided, write one specific benefit of competence for each of the economic activities listed.

Economic Activity	Benefits of Competence	
	For Individuals	**For the Economy**
Earning	standard of living rises	GDP rises
Spending	allowed to make own spending choices	helps bring about prosperity and avoid recession
Saving	increase financial well-being	money is loaned to other individuals and businesses
Borrowing	pay for major purchases	increases amount of money in circulation
Insuring	protection against financial losses	strengthens overall economic stability
Investing	increase future economic security	pay for a large share of business growth and activity
Paying taxes	provides services citizens want and need	spending tax dollars stimulates the economy

Trace Your Dollars

Activity D   Name _______________________________

Chapter 3   Date ________________ Period _______________

Try to name at least five businesses and individuals who benefit when you use your dollars in each of the following ways. Trace your money from the receiver of the money to the original producer or supplier of the goods or services you are buying. Remember to mention middle persons, such as advertisers, distributors, packers, and processors. An example has been given to help you.

1. You buy a $75 coat at a clothing store. Beneficiaries include: *the store, store employee(s), employee's family, packer, distributor, manufacturer of coat, manufacturer of fabric, manufacturers of notions used in coat, designer*

2. You spend $10 at the movie theater for ticket, candy, popcorn, and drink. Beneficiaries include:
   (List five:) theater, theater employees, actors, movie studio, candy makers, candy advertisers, popcorn manufacturers, soft drink company, cup manufacturers

3. You spend $45 for CDs and DVDs. Beneficiaries are:
   (List five:) movie studios, disc manufacturers, packaging manufacturers, advertisers, actors, musicians, music label, music label employees

4. You pay $150 for an airline ticket. Beneficiaries include:
   (List five:) pilots, flight attendants, maintenance crew, airline's airport personnel, plane manufacturers, advertisers, airline company, subsidiary airport personnel

5. You buy a $500 certificate of deposit at a local bank. Beneficiaries include:
   (List five:) the bank corporation, bank employees, companies to whom the money is loaned, employees at companies to which the money is loaned, bank advertisers, the economy

6. You pay $1,200 for a computer and word processing software. Beneficiaries are:
   (List five:) computer manufacturer, manufacturer employees, software programmers, software company, store, store employees, computer advertisers, software advertisers, packaging designers

7. You spend $55 at the supermarket. Beneficiaries include:
   (List five:) supermarket corporation, supermarket employees, food companies, food distributors, food package designers, food manufacturers or farmers, supermarket advertisers, food advertisers

Chapter 4
The Global Economy
Comparative Advantage

Activity A

Chapter 4

Name ________________________________

Date _________________ Period ______________

Darnell and Jane bake bread and cookies and sell them at the farmer's market every Saturday. Darnell's output is 6 dozen cookies in 1 hour and 6 loaves of bread in 2 hours (or 3 loaves an hour). Jane's output is 6 dozen cookies in 4 hours (or 1.5 dozen cookies an hour). She makes 6 loaves of bread in 3 hours (or 2 loaves an hour).

1. If Darnell works three hours and Jane works seven hours, how many cookies and bread loaves will they make total? _12 dozen cookies and 12 loaves of bread—Darnell will make 6 dozen cookies in 1 hour and 6 loaves of bread in 2 hours. Jane will make 6 dozen cookies in 4 hours and 6 loaves of bread in 3 hours._

2. A. Calculate each person's opportunity cost of making 6 dozen cookies. _Darnell's opportunity cost is 1 hour or the 3 loaves of bread he could have made in an hour if he did not make cookies. Jane's opportunity cost is 4 hours or the 8 loaves of bread she could have made in 4 hours if she did not make cookies._

   B. In cookie making, who has the comparative advantage? Explain. _Darnell has the lower opportunity cost so he has the comparative advantage._

3. A. Calculate each person's opportunity cost of making 6 loaves of bread. _Darnell's opportunity cost is 2 hours or the 12 dozen cookies he could have made in the 2 hours it takes to make the bread. Jane's opportunity cost is 3 hours, or the 4.5 dozen cookies she could have made in 3 hours if she did not make bread._

   B. In bread making, who has the comparative advantage? Explain. _Jane has the lower opportunity cost so she has the comparative advantage._

4. Darnell is more productive than Jane in both items. If he and Jane work together and specialize, can they increase total production of both items? Explain. _Yes. If Darnell spends the same 3 hours and makes only cookies at 6 dozen per hour, he will produce 18 dozen cookies. If Jane spends the same 7 hours and makes only bread at 2 loaves per hour, she will produce 14 loaves of bread. They have increased their total output by 6 dozen cookies and 2 loaves of bread. This benefits both._

Understanding Migration: An Interview

Activity B

Chapter 4

Name ______________________________

Date _________________ Period _______________

Interview someone you know who was born in a foreign country but now lives in the United States. This person can be a parent, grandparent, friend, neighbor, or local businessperson. Ask the following questions and write down a summary of the person's response. Share your interview with your class. (Answers are student response.)

How long have you lived in the U.S.? ______________________________

How old were you when you came to the U.S.? ______________________________

What country did you live in before you came to the U.S.? ______________________________

Did you live in a rural or urban area, a village, or a city? ______________________________

____

Why did you leave that country? ______________________________

____

____

Can you describe the government and economic system of your country of origin? ______________________________

____

____

In your opinion, what are some of the biggest problems there? ______________________________

____

____

How do economic opportunities in the U.S. compare with those in your country of origin? ______________________________

____

____

Do you keep in touch with people in that country? If so, how? ______________________________

____

____

What surprised you most about the U.S.? ______________________________

____

____

What have you found most challenging about making the move? ______________________________

____

Imports Scavenger Hunt

Activity C

Chapter 4

Name _________________________________

Date _________________ Period _________________

Some common products are listed below. Find an example of each, either in your home or a store, that is labeled with a country of origin. This information may be listed on a package label, an attached tag, the product box, or the manufacturer's Web site. Write the brand name of the product, a short description, and its country of origin. Answer the questions that follow.

Consumer electronics product—brand name: (Answers are student response.) _________________

    Description: _________________________________

____

____

    Country of origin: _________________________________

Fresh or dried fruit—brand name: _________________________________

    Description: _________________________________

____

____

    Country of origin: _________________________________

Shoes—brand name: _________________________________

    Description: _________________________________

____

____

    Country of origin: _________________________________

T-shirt—brand name: _________________________________

    Description: _________________________________

____

____

    Country of origin: _________________________________

Children's toy—brand name: _________________________________

    Description: _________________________________

____

____

    Country of origin: _________________________________

(Continued)

Name____

Candy—brand name: (Answers are student response.)________________________

   Description: ____

____

____

   Country of origin: ____

Personal care product—brand name: ____

   Description: ____

____

____

   Country of origin: ____

Book—brand name: ____

   Description: ____

____

____

   Country of origin: ____

Furniture—brand name: ____

   Description: ____

____

____

   Country of origin: ____

Sports equipment—brand name: ____

   Description: ____

____

____

   Country of origin: ____

Pet food—brand name:____

   Description: ____

____

____

   Country of origin: ____

How many of the products were made in the U.S.? ____

How many were imported from a foreign country? ____

Were you surprised by your results? Why or why not? ____

____

____

Making Choices

Activity A   Name ____

Chapter 5   Date _________________   Period _______________

Ranking your values calls for making choices. Read the following list of values. Add any others that you consider important. Then rank them in the order of importance to you. (Begin by writing the number *1* beside the most important.) Then answer the question below.

(Rankings are student response.)

______	Adventure	______	Family
______	Justice	______	Education
______	Nature	______	Popularity
______	Music	______	Material possessions
______	Friendship	______	Contentment
______	Leisure time	______	Personal security
______	Art	______	Religion
______	Peace	______	Good health
______	Self-esteem	______	____________________
______	Love	______	____________________

How do your most important values influence the choices that you make? Give at least three specific examples. (Answers are student response.) ____

____

____

____

____

____

____

____

____

Your Resources

Name ___________________________________

Date _______________ Period _______________

Identify and briefly describe your human and nonhuman resources. Then analyze your list and answer the questions below.

Your human resources:

__(Student response.)____

____

____

____

____

____

The nonhuman resources available to you:

__(Student response.)____

____

____

____

____

1. Which resources are in short supply? ___(Student response.)__________

____

2. Which resources are plentiful?___(Student response.)________________

____

3. Which resources do you use frequently? ___(Student response.)________

____

4. Which could you use more effectively to meet your goals?___(Student response.)____

____

Psychological Aspects of Money

Name ___________________________________

Date ______________________ Period ________________

Complete the following statements. Consider your answers and what they reveal about your needs, wants, values, goals, and standards concerning money. There are no right or wrong answers.

1. Four important things money *cannot* do are (Student response.) ___________________

   ____

   ____

2. Four important things money *can* do are (Student response.) _________________

   ____

   ____

3. A big waste of money is (Student response.) ________________________________

   ____

4. To me, buying a quality product means (Student response.) _________________

   ____

5. When I have no money, I feel (Student response.) __________________________

   ____

6. When I have a little extra money, I usually (Student response.) ___________

   ____

7. One big problem I have handling money is (Student response.) ______________

   ____

8. If someone gave me $500 to spend, I would (Student response.) _____________

   ____

9. Some things that I think are more important than having enough money are ___________
   (Student response.)

   ____

(Continued)

Name _______________________________________

10. To me, having enough money means (Student response.)
____
____

11. Three things for which I would be willing to make a charitable contribution are_______________
(Student response.)
____

12. Three things for which I would be willing to save money are (Student response.)
____
____

13. The five things I buy most frequently with my own money are (Student response.)
____
____
____

14. I think people are overly concerned about money when they (Student response.)
____
____

15. I place great importance on purchases such as (Student response.)
____
____

16. If I really needed to save money, I would spend less on (Student response.)
____
____

17. The biggest mistake I ever made with money was (Student response.)
____
____

18. I would only loan money to someone who (Student response.)
____
____

19. If I loaned money to a friend who wouldn't repay it, I would (Student response.)
____
____

Your Financial Tendencies

Name ______________________________

Date ________________   Period ______________

Analyze your financial tendencies by circling the number between one and ten that is closest to your position on the following items. There are no right or wrong answers.

(Ratings are student response.)

SPENDING

Save every   Spend every
penny   penny

1   2   3   4   5   6   7   8   9   10

CREDIT

Never use it   Charge everything

1   2   3   4   5   6   7   8   9   10

GIVING

Never give   Donate to
money away   every cause

1   2   3   4   5   6   7   8   9   10

EARNING

Constantly looking for   Give little or no thought
ways to earn money   to earning money

1   2   3   4   5   6   7   8   9   10

FINANCIAL PLANNING

Too busy planning for   Let the future take
tomorrow to enjoy today   care of itself

1   2   3   4   5   6   7   8   9   10

MATERIAL POSSESSIONS

No interest in   Can't get enough
owning things   merchandise

1   2   3   4   5   6   7   8   9   10

(Continued)

Name ____

SHOPPING SKILLS

Shop carefully to
avoid mistakes   Buy on impulse

1   2   3   4   5   6   7   8   9   10

CONSUMER PROBLEMS

Would never complain   Rather die than
about anything   get ripped-off

1   2   3   4   5   6   7   8   9   10

On the lines below describe your financial tendencies based on your responses.

(Descriptions are student response.)

____

____

____

____

____

____

____

Rational Decision Making

Activity E

Name

Chapter 5

Date   Period

Briefly describe a situation in your life that calls for a decision. Then apply the decision-making process to this situation.

Situation: (Student response.)

1. What is the problem? (Student response.)

2. What are the alternatives? (Student response.)

3. What is the best alternative? (Student response.)

4. How can you apply the best alternative? (Student response.)

5. How would you evaluate your solution or decision? (Student response.)

Planning

Activity F

Chapter 5

Name ___________________________

Date ________________ Period ___________

Planning is an important phase in the management process. Choose a goal that you want to reach. Then complete a plan to achieve that goal.

Goal: _(Student response.)_ ___________________________

Obstacles to Achieving Goal	Available Resources to Achieve Goal
(Obstacles are student response.)	(Resources are student response.)

Plan: Describe how you could use your available resources to overcome obstacles and reach your goal.

(Student response.)

Chapter 6
Personal Finance: An Overview

Your Money Management Style

<table>
<tr><td>Activity A</td><td>Name ______________________________</td></tr>
<tr><td>Chapter 6</td><td>Date ________________ Period ____________</td></tr>
</table>

Answer *yes* or *no* to the following questions.   (Answers are student response.)

______ 1. Can you give a reasonably detailed account of how you spent your money over the last two weeks?

______ 2. Do you know within two dollars how much money you have with you at this moment?

______ 3. Do you know within five dollars how much money you will have to spend over the next week?

______ 4. Do you have a detailed money management plan?

______ 5. Can you describe the financial goals you want to reach within the next three years?

______ 6. Are you usually satisfied with your purchases?

______ 7. Do you normally consider both the dollar price and the opportunity cost of items you buy?

______ 8. Do you know some ways to use nonmoney resources to stretch your dollars?

______ 9. Do you keep receipts, records, and money management materials together in a convenient place?

______ 10. Do you save regularly for things that are important to you?

______ 11. Do you plan ahead for major expected expenses?

______ 12. Do you have any money in savings or reserve for unexpected expenses and emergencies?

______ 13. Do you ever think about ways to earn money and qualify for jobs?

______ 14. Do you evaluate and revise your money management plans and spending habits periodically?

______ 15. Do you make a point of learning from your spending mistakes?

Give yourself seven points for every honest *yes*. If your score is less than 70, you need to sharpen your money management skills.

Complete this statement: (Answers are student response.)

My score of ______ reflects ____

____

I could improve my money management style by (Student response.) ______

____

                    31

Stick to the Plan

Activity B   Name _______________________________

Chapter 6   Date __________________ Period __________

Complete this money management plan by listing your expected income, planned expenses, and remaining balance. Then answer the questions below.

Money Management Plan

Income	Weekly	Monthly	Yearly
Allowance	(Answers are student response.)		
Wages			
Gifts			
Other			
Total Income	$	$	$
Expenses (List)			
Fixed:			
Variable:			
Discretionary:			
Total Expenses	$	$	$
Balance (Subtract total expenses from total income.)	$	$	$

1. How can planning help you manage your money? (Student response.)

   ____

   ____

2. What are some steps you can take when your remaining balance is negative—when you are spending more than you have? (Student response.)

   ____

   ____

Tracking Your Money

Activity C   Name _________________________________

Chapter 6   Date _______________ Period _______________

In the space below, track your routine spending for one week. List your fixed and variable expenses.

Amounts Spent								(Answers are student response.)
Items	**Day 1**	**Day 2**	**Day 3**	**Day 4**	**Day 5**	**Day 6**	**Day 7**	**Total per item**
Fixed expenses:								
(Answers are student response.)								
Variable expenses:								
(Answers are student response.)								
Totals per day								

(Continued)

Name ____

Now, list and estimate the discretionary expenses you anticipate over the next six months.

Item	Amount	Date Payable
(Answers are student response.)		
Total		

Take a careful look at your record of spending and your estimate of upcoming discretionary expenses. Then answer the following questions.

1. What, if any, changes would you like to make in your spending habits? _______________
    (Student response.) ____

    ____

2. What items would you cut or eliminate if you had to spend less? (Student response.) ______

    ____

    ____

3. What would you add to your spending list if you had more money to spend? ____________
    (Student response.) ____

    ____

4. In what way do you think expense items and amounts will change during your first year out of
    high school? (Student response.) ____

    ____

    ____

    five years from now? (Student response.) ____

    ____

    ____

5. What did you learn by tracking your money? (Student response.) ___________________

    ____

    ____

    ____

Your Net Worth

Name _______________________________________

Date _________________   Period _______________

Determine your net worth by completing this financial statement.

Financial Statement
(Answers are student response.)

Assets

Liquid Assets:

Cash on hand $ _____

Cash in savings, checking,
and money market accounts   _____

Cash value of insurance   _____

Other   _____

Total Liquid Assets . . . . $ _____

Investment Assets:

Stocks and bonds $ _____

Mutual funds   _____

Individual Retirement Accounts   _____

Other   _____

Total Investment Assets . . . . $ _____

Use Assets: (market values)

Auto $ _____

Home   _____

Furniture and equipment   _____

Other   _____

Total Use Assets . . . . $ _____

Total Assets . . . . $ _____

Liabilities

Current Liabilities:

Credit cards and charge account
balances due $ _____

Taxes due   _____

Other   _____

Total Current Liabilities . . . . $ _____

Long-term Liabilities:

Auto loan $ _____

Home mortgage   _____

Other   _____ .

Total Long-term Liabilities . . . . $ _____

Total Liabilities. . . . . $ _____

Net Worth (total assets less total liabilities) . . . . $ _____

Life Cycle Planning

Name _______________________________

Date _________________ Period _______________

In the space provided, describe typical characteristics and financial activities for different stages in the family life cycle. Discuss in class the progression from stage to stage and the differences for variations in the cycle, such as single parent families, single individuals, divorced or separated people, and childless couples.

Stage in Cycle	Financial Characteristics	Financial Activities
Beginning	Income starts low and gradually increases. Two-income couples enjoy the benefits of combined incomes. People who marry later may have higher incomes.	education, college loans, home furnishings, insurance, down payment on a home, an auto, savings, contributions to a retirement fund
Expanding	Job advancement may bring higher income. If one spouse leaves the workforce to raise children, income declines. At the same time, expenses increase.	child-related expenses, a larger home, expanded insurance protection, an educational fund for children, drawing up a will
Developing	Income and expenses both climb.	school-age child-related expenses such as larger clothing budget, sports and hobby equipment, lessons and tutoring, allowances, and savings for future education; a second car; housing, insurance, taxes, education, savings, and retirement planning
Launching	Job advancements often bring higher incomes, and earnings may peak.	college expenses, retirement savings, care for aging parents
Aging	Earnings level off.	health and nursing-care costs, reliable health insurance and long-term care insurance, declining living expenses, estate planning

Chapter 7
Income and Taxes

Spending Tax Dollars

Activity A   Name _______________________________________

Chapter 7   Date ___________________ Period ________________

Visit the Government Printing Office Budget Website (www.gpoaccess.gov/usbudget). Browse annual budget documents and use the summary tables to complete the following charts. Then answer the questions that follow.

Federal Government Receipts by Source (in billions of dollars)			
Sources of Income	10 Years Ago	5 Years Ago	Last Year
Individual income tax		(Chart answers are student response.)	
Corporate income tax			
Social Security and other insurance and retirement contributions			
Excise taxes			
Estate and gift taxes			
Customs duties			
Miscellaneous receipts			
Other			
Total Income			

Federal Government Outlays for Last Year		
Outlay	Dollars (in billions)	Percent of Total Outlays
	(Chart answers are student response.)	
Total Outlays		

(Continued)

Name _______________________________________

1. How have amounts of income coming from various sources changed over the years? _________
   (Student response.)
   ____
   ____
   ____

2. Did the government receive enough income last year to cover outlays? (Student response.)
   ____

3. What are some ways government could increase revenues? (Student response.)
   ____
   ____
   ____

4 What percent of last year's outlays went to discretionary expenses? (Student response.)
   ____

5. What percent of last year's outlays went to mandatory expenses? (Student response.)
   ____

6. Which outlays do you think government should cut back on in order to reduce spending?
   Explain your answer. (Student response.)
   ____
   ____
   ____

7. Which outlays would you be willing to pay higher taxes to support? Explain your answer. _____
   (Student response.)
   ____
   ____
   ____

8. Do you feel the tax system is fair? Explain your answer. (Student response.)
   ____
   ____
   ____

Income Tax Return

Activity B   Name _______________________________

Chapter 7   Date ________________ Period __________

You are going to prepare Justine Davis's tax return. Use the following information, Justine's Form W-2, and the tax table below to complete the Form 1040EZ on the next page.

- Justine does not want $3.00 to go to the Presidential Election Campaign Fund.
- Justine's taxable interest income is $31.00.
- No one else can claim Justine on a tax return.
- Justine is not eligible for the earned income credit or recovery rebate credit.

a Employee's social security number		
123-45-6789	OMB No. 1545-0008	Safe, accurate, FAST! Use IRS e-file — Visit the IRS website at www.irs.gov/efile.

b Employer identification number (EIN)	1 Wages, tips, other compensation	2 Federal income tax withheld
32-1234567	37558.26	3917.58

c Employer's name, address, and ZIP code	3 Social security wages	4 Social security tax withheld
XYZ Corporation 864 N. Spring Road Chicago, IL 60606	37558.26	2873.21
	5 Medicare wages and tips	6 Medicare tax withheld
		550.95
	7 Social security tips	8 Allocated tips

d Control number	9 Advance EIC payment	10 Dependent care benefits

e Employee's first name and initial — Last name — Suff.	11 Nonqualified plans	12a See instructions for box 12
Justine Davis 2319 W. Carlson Drive Chicago, IL 60600	13 Statutory employee ☐ Retirement plan ☐ Third-party sick pay ☐	12b
	14 Other	12c
		12d

f Employee's address and ZIP code

15 State	Employer's state ID number	16 State wages, tips, etc.	17 State income tax	18 Local wages, tips, etc.	19 Local income tax	20 Locality name
IL	XX-XXXXXXX	37558.26	1767.08			

Form **W-2** Wage and Tax Statement **20XX** Department of the Treasury—Internal Revenue Service

Copy B—To Be Filed With Employee's FEDERAL Tax Return.
This information is being furnished to the Internal Revenue Service.

If Form 1040EZ, line 6, is –		And you are –		If Form 1040EZ, line 6, is –		And you are –		If Form 1040EZ, line 6, is –		And you are –		If Form 1040EZ, line 6, is –		And you are –	
At least	But less than	Single	Married filing jointly	At least	But less than	Single	Married filing jointly	At least	But less than	Single	Married filing jointly	At least	But less than	Single	Married filing jointly
		Your tax is –				Your tax is –				Your tax is –				Your tax is –	
22,000				**25,000**				**28,000**				**31,000**			
22,000	22,050	2,903	2,501	25,000	25,050	3,353	2,951	28,000	28,050	3,803	3,401	31,000	31,050	4,253	3,851
22,050	22,100	2,910	2,509	25,050	25,100	3,360	2,959	28,050	28,100	3,810	3,409	31,050	31,100	4,260	3,859
22,100	22,150	2,918	2,516	25,100	25,150	3,368	2,966	28,100	28,150	3,818	3,416	31,100	31,150	4,268	3,866
22,150	22,200	2,925	2,524	25,150	25,200	3,375	2,974	28,150	28,200	3,825	3,424	31,150	31,200	4,275	3,874
22,200	22,250	2,933	2,531	25,200	25,250	3,383	2,981	28,200	28,250	3,833	3,431	31,200	31,250	4,283	3,881
22,250	22,300	2,940	2,539	25,250	25,300	3,390	2,989	28,250	28,300	3,840	3,439	31,250	31,300	4,290	3,889
22,300	22,350	2,948	2,546	25,300	25,350	3,398	2,996	28,300	28,350	3,848	3,446	31,300	31,350	4,298	3,896
22,350	22,400	2,955	2,554	25,350	25,400	3,405	3,004	28,350	28,400	3,855	3,454	31,350	31,400	4,305	3,904
22,400	22,450	2,963	2,561	25,400	25,450	3,413	3,011	28,400	28,450	3,863	3,461	31,400	31,450	4,313	3,911
22,450	22,500	2,970	2,569	25,450	25,500	3,420	3,019	28,450	28,500	3,870	3,469	31,450	31,500	4,320	3,919
22,500	22,550	2,978	2,576	25,500	25,550	3,428	3,026	28,500	28,550	3,878	3,476	31,500	31,550	4,328	3,926
22,550	22,600	2,985	2,584	25,550	25,600	3,435	3,034	28,550	28,600	3,885	3,484	31,550	31,600	4,335	3,934
22,600	22,650	2,993	2,591	25,600	25,650	3,443	3,041	28,600	28,650	3,893	3,491	31,600	31,650	4,343	3,941

(Continued)

Name_______________________________________

Department of the Treasury—Internal Revenue Service

Form 1040EZ

Income Tax Return for Single and Joint Filers With No Dependents (99) **20XX**

OMB No. 1545-0074

Label (See page 9.)

Use the IRS label.

Otherwise, please print or type.

Presidential Election Campaign (page 9)

L A B E L H E R E

Your first name and initial	Last name
Justine	Davis

If a joint return, spouse's first name and initial — Last name

Home address (number and street). If you have a P.O. box, see page 9. — Apt. no.

2319 W. Carlson Drive

City, town or post office, state, and ZIP code. If you have a foreign address, see page 9.

Chicago, IL 60600

Your social security number

123 45 6789

Spouse's social security number

▲ You **must** enter your SSN(s) above. ▲

Checking a box below will not change your tax or refund.

Check here if you, or your spouse if a joint return, want $3 to go to this fund . . . ▶ ☐ **You**   ☐ **Spouse**

Income

Attach Form(s) W-2 here.

Enclose, but do not attach, any payment.

1	Wages, salaries, and tips. This should be shown in box 1 of your Form(s) W-2. Attach your Form(s) W-2.	1	37,558 26
2	Taxable interest. If the total is over $1,500, you cannot use Form 1040EZ.	2	31 00
3	Unemployment compensation and Alaska Permanent Fund dividends (see page 11).	3	
4	Add lines 1, 2, and 3. This is your **adjusted gross income.**	4	37,589 26
5	If someone can claim you (or your spouse if a joint return) as a dependent, check the applicable box(es) below and enter the amount from the worksheet on back. ☐ **You** ☐ **Spouse** If no one can claim you (or your spouse if a joint return), enter $8,950 if **single;** $17,900 if **married filing jointly.** See back for explanation.	5	8,950 00
6	Subtract line 5 from line 4. If line 5 is larger than line 4, enter -0-. This is your **taxable income.** ▶	6	28,639 26

Payments and tax

7	Federal income tax withheld from box 2 of your Form(s) W-2.	7	3,917 58
8a	**Earned income credit (EIC)** (see page 12).	8a	
b	Nontaxable combat pay election. 8b		
9	Recovery rebate credit (see worksheet on pages 17 and 18).	9	
10	Add lines 7, 8a, and 9. These are your **total payments.** ▶	10	3,917 58
11	**Tax.** Use the amount on **line 6 above** to find your tax in the tax table on pages 28–36 of the booklet. Then, enter the tax from the table on this line.	11	3,893 00

Refund

Have it directly deposited! See page 18 and fill in 12b, 12c, and 12d or Form 8888.

12a	If line 10 is larger than line 11, subtract line 11 from line 10. This is your **refund.** If Form 8888 is attached, check here ▶ ☐	12a	24 58

▶ **b** Routing number ☐☐☐☐☐☐☐☐☐   ▶ **c** Type: ☐ Checking ☐ Savings

▶ **d** Account number ☐☐☐☐☐☐☐☐☐☐☐☐☐☐☐☐☐

Amount you owe

13   If line 11 is larger than line 10, subtract line 10 from line 11. This is the **amount you owe.** For details on how to pay, see page 19. ▶ 13

Third party designee

Do you want to allow another person to discuss this return with the IRS (see page 20)? ☐ **Yes.** Complete the following. ☑ **No**

Designee's name ▶   Phone no. ▶ ( )   Personal identification number (PIN) ▶ ☐☐☐☐☐

Sign here

Joint return? See page 6.

Keep a copy for your records.

Under penalties of perjury, I declare that I have examined this return, and to the best of my knowledge and belief, it is true, correct, and accurately lists all amounts and sources of income I received during the tax year. Declaration of preparer (other than the taxpayer) is based on all information of which the preparer has any knowledge.

Your signature	Date	Your occupation	Daytime phone number
Justine Davis	3/21/XX	Office Professional	(789)123-4567
Spouse's signature. If a joint return, **both** must sign.	Date	Spouse's occupation	

Paid preparer's use only

Preparer's signature ▶	Date	Check if self-employed ☐	Preparer's SSN or PTIN
Firm's name (or yours if self-employed), address, and ZIP code ▶		EIN Phone no. ( )	

For Disclosure, Privacy Act, and Paperwork Reduction Act Notice, see page 37.   Cat. No. 11329W   Form **1040EZ** (2008)

Tax Facts

Name ____

Date ____________________   Period ________________

Complete the following statements about taxes. Fill in the puzzle with the correct words to discover a service that taxes provide.

	1						
1	d	i	r	e	c	t
2	p	r	o	g	r	e	s	s	i	v	e
3	p e r s o n a l i n c o m e
4	r	e	g	r	e	s	s	i	v	e
5	s	a	l	e	s
6	e	s	t	a	t	e
7	g	i	f	t
8	e	x	c	i	s	e
9	p e r s o n a l p r o p e r t y
10	i	n	d	i	r	e	c	t

1. _____ taxes are paid directly to the government by taxpayers.

2. _____ taxes take a higher percentage from the rich than from the poor.

3. A tax on the amount of money a person receives from wages, tips, bonuses, interest, and dividends is _____ _____ tax.

4. _____ taxes take a lower percentage from the rich and a higher percentage from the poor.

5. A purchase tax levied by state and local governments on retail sales of certain goods and services is _____ tax.

6. _____ tax is imposed by the federal government on assets left by an individual at the time of his or her death.

7. When someone donates or gives a gift over a certain amount, he or she will have to pay _____ tax.

8. _____ tax is levied by federal and state governments on the sale and transfer of certain luxury items.

9. A tax based on the items such as cars, boats, and furniture is called _____ tax.

10. _____ taxes are imposed on one person or entity and paid by another.

Social Security

Name ______________________________

Date ____________________ Period ______________________

In the future, there may be changes in Social Security legislation due to financial problems. Listed below are some possible solutions to ensure the financial soundness of the program. Discuss these in class. (You may add a solution of your own.) Then list advantages and disadvantages of each solution and name the group of citizens most affected by each action.

Action	Advantages	Disadvantages	Group Affected
Reduce the automatic cost-of-living allowance (COLAs) increases in benefits.		(Chart answers are student response.)	
Cut benefits for higher-income recipients			
Raise the retirement age.			
Increase Social Security tax contributions.			
Permit individuals to invest a portion of their Social Security taxes in personal retirement accounts.			
Other:			

Comparing Financial Institutions

Activity A

Chapter 8

Name _______________________________________

Date ___________________ Period _______________

Visit at lease three financial institutions in your area. Use the following chart to indicate the conveniences and services offered by each.

	Name of Institution:		Name of Institution:		Name of Institution:	
	Yes	No	Yes	No	Yes	No
CONVENIENCE Does it have: *(Answers are student response.)*						
convenient hours and location?						
drive-up services?						
an ATM on the premises?						
ATMs at other locations?						
automatic bill paying?						
telephone transfers?						
online banking?						
helpful personnel?						
FINANCIAL SERVICES Does it offer:						
checking accounts?						
savings accounts?						
cashier's checks?						
money orders?						
traveler's checks?						
safe-deposit boxes?						
financial counseling?						
brokerage services?						

Banking Basics

Name ______________________________________

Date _________________   Period _______________

Follow the instructions to complete the two financial transactions.

Signature Card:

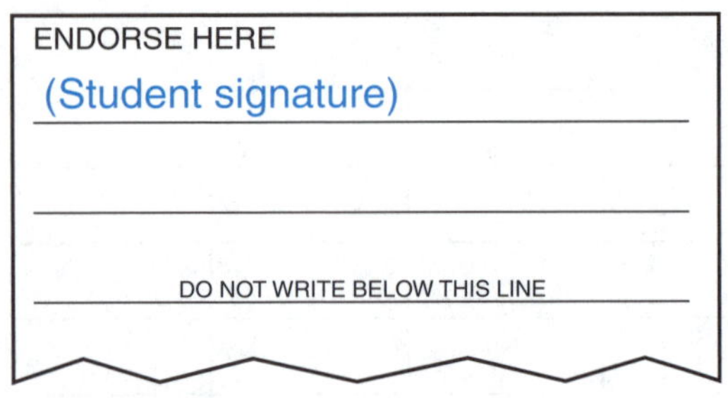

The signature card is used to protect your account from forgery. Complete the signature card at left. Sign your name the same way you plan to sign your checks.

Endorsing Checks:

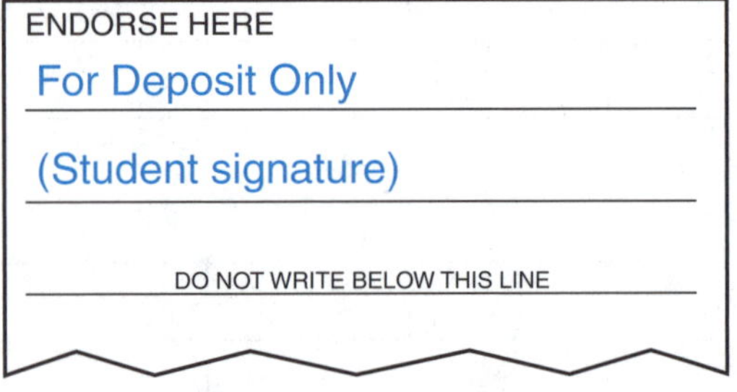

Endorse this check with a *blank endorsement*.

Use a *restrictive endorsement* stating "For Deposit Only."

Use a *special endorsement* to transfer this check to Gary Johnson.

Checking Accounts

Activity C

Chapter 8

Name _______________________________

Date _______________ Period _______________

Pretend you are Thomas or Mary Anderson and you have a checking account at a local bank. Complete the following transactions.

Making a deposit:

You want to deposit $20.00 in currency, $7.49 in coins, a $54.30 check, and a $93.25 check. Using this information and today's date, fill out this deposit slip.

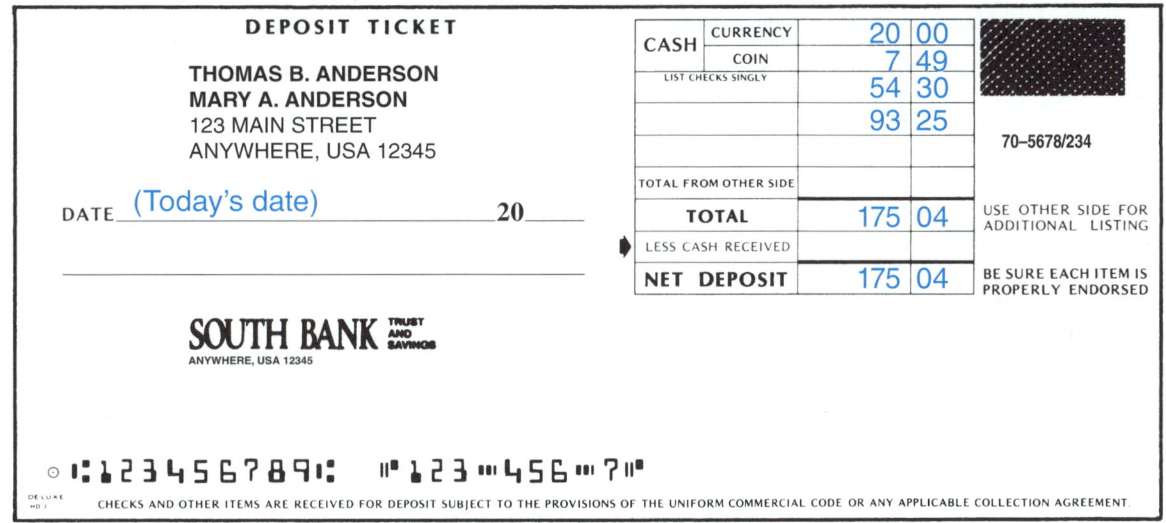

Writing a check:

Write a check for $67.48 to pay for car repairs at Jim's Car Care Shop. Use today's date.

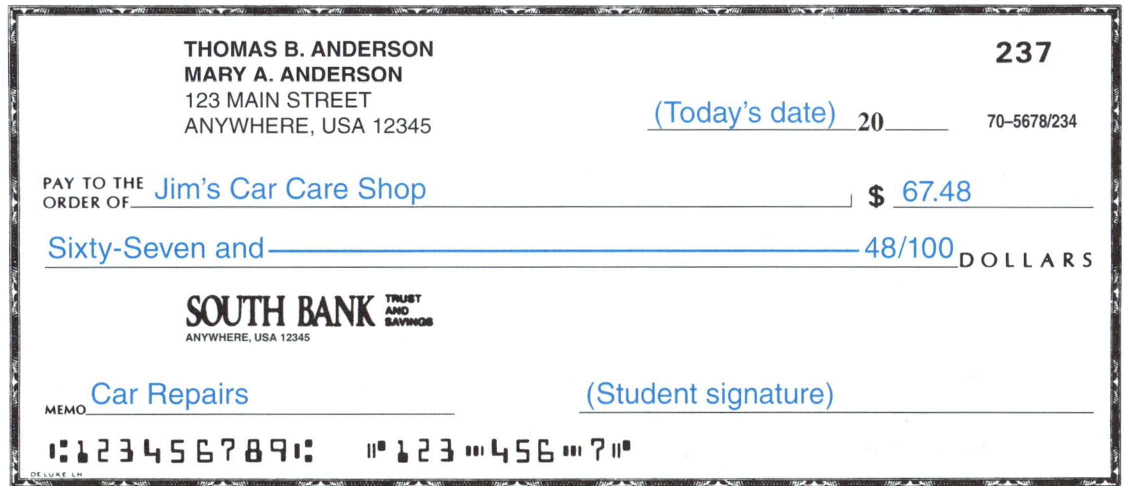

Name____

Filling out a check register:

Record your deposit and check for car repairs in this check register. Your previous balance was $115.45.

20___		BE SURE TO DEDUCT ANY PER ITEM CHARGES, SERVICE CHARGES, OR FEES THAT MAY APPLY						
DATE	NUMBER	TRANSACTION DESCRIPTION	(+ OR –) OTHER	✓ T	(+) AMOUNT OF DEPOSIT	(–) AMOUNT OF PAYMENT OR WITHDRAWAL	BALANCE FORWARD	115 45
(Date)		Deposit			175 04		290 49	
(Date)	237	Jim's Car Care Shop	67 48				223 01	

Balancing a checkbook:

Your bank statement shows a closing balance of $200.21. The deposit you made earlier in this activity is not shown on the statement. The check you wrote earlier in this activity is not shown on the statement. You have four additional outstanding checks: $41.32 (#224), $14.97 (#226), $20.00 (#231), and $8.47 (#236). Use this information to fill in this balancing worksheet. The balance on the worksheet should be the same as the balance above in the check register.

BALANCING WORKSHEET

CHECKS OUTSTANDING
(Written but not shown on statement because not yet received by Bank.)

MONTH (Current date) , 20_____

NO.	$	
224	41	32
226	14	97
231	20	00
236	8	47
237	67	48
TOTAL	152	24

BANK BALANCE $ 200.21
shown on this statement

ADD +

$ 175.04

DEPOSITS made but not shown on statement because made or received after date of this statement.

TOTAL $ 375.25

SUBTRACT –

CHECKS OUTSTANDING ..... $ 152.24

BALANCE .... $ 223.01
The above balance should be the same as the up-to-date balance in your checkbook.

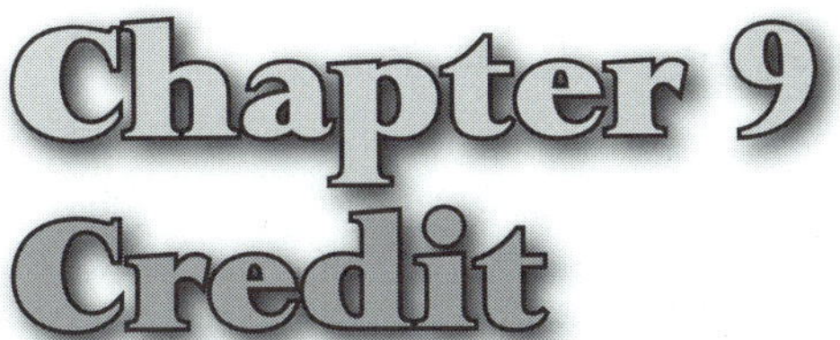

Chapter 9
Credit

Your Credit Opinions

Activity A

Chapter 9

Name _______________________________

Date ___________________ Period _______________

Complete the following statements related to the use of credit. (There are no right or wrong answers.)

1. If I owed a friend $50 and could not pay, I would (Student response.) _______________

2. If a friend owed me $50 and could not pay, I would (Student response.) _______________

3. Three things I would not use credit for are (Student response.) _______________

4. Three things I would be willing to use credit to buy are (Student response.) _______________

5. I think the use of credit becomes excessive when (Student response.) _______________

6. I think the greatest cause of credit problems is (Student response.) _______________

7. If I lost a wallet with several credit cards in it, I would (Student response.) _______________

8. If I received a bill for merchandise I did not buy or if I was *overcharged* for something I bought on credit, I would (Student response.) _______________

9. If I received a bill and was undercharged for merchandise I bought on credit, I would ___________
    (Student response.)

10. If I applied for credit and was refused because of a false credit report, I would _______________
    (Student response.)

11. The best thing about using credit is (Student response.) _______________

12. If someone doesn't pay a bill, I think the creditor should be able to (Student response.) _______________

Credit Worthiness Survey

Activity B

Chapter 9

Name _______________________________

Date _______________ Period _______________

Below are some questions creditors are likely to consider when you apply for credit. Answer yes or no to the questions. Then rate yourself as a credit applicant as explained below.

______ 1. Do you have a steady job? (Answers are student response.)

______ 2. Do you have a good employment record?

______ 3. Do you own property or possessions of value?

______ 4. Do you have a steady income from a reliable source?

______ 5. Do you pay bills promptly?

______ 6. Do you keep reasonably complete, accurate financial records?

______ 7. Do you take care of your obligations?

______ 8. Do you have credit accounts you have managed well?

______ 9. Do you have a savings account to which you make regular deposits?

______ 10. Do you have a well-managed checking account?

______ 11. Can you provide bank and other character references?

______ 12. Are you considered financially responsible?

______ 13. Do other people think of you as trustworthy and reliable?

______ 14. Do you understand the details and mechanics of using credit?

______ 15. Do you manage your money reasonably well?

Give yourself 1 point for each yes answer. Score your credit worthiness as follows: 15-13 Desirable; 12-10 Acceptable; 9-7 Questionable; 6-4 Poor; 3-0 Unacceptable.

My score is _________. My credit worthiness is _(Student response.)_________________

To improve my credit rating, I need to _(Student response.)_______________________

____

____

____

____

____

____

____

____

Credit Application

<table>
<tr><td>Activity C</td><td>Name ______________________________</td></tr>
<tr><td>Chapter 9</td><td>Date ____________ Period ____________</td></tr>
</table>

Complete the following credit application form. Answer the questions that follow.

(Form answers are student response.)

BELK CREDIT APPLICATION

EMPLOYEE NO.		DATE	
	Type of Account Requested: ☐ INDIVIDUAL ☐ JOINT		

PLEASE TELL US ABOUT YOURSELF

FIRST NAME (TITLES OPTIONAL)	MIDDLE INITIAL	LAST NAME		AGE
STREET ADDRESS (IF P.O. BOX — PLEASE GIVE STREET ADDRESS)		CITY	STATE	ZIP

☐ OWN ☐ LIVE WITH RELATIVE ☐ RENT ☐ OTHER	MONTHLY PAYMENT $	YEARS AT PRESENT ADDRESS	HOME PHONE NO. ( )	NO. OF DEPENDENTS
PREVIOUS ADDRESS		CITY	STATE ZIP	HOW LONG

NAME OF NEAREST RELATIVE NOT LIVING WITH YOU	RELATIONSHIP	PHONE NO. ( )	
ADDRESS	CITY		STATE

NOW TELL US ABOUT YOUR JOB

EMPLOYER OR INCOME SOURCE	POSITION/TITLE	HOW LONG EMPLOYED YRS. MOS.	MONTHLY INCOME $
EMPLOYER'S ADDRESS	CITY	STATE	TYPE OF BUSINESS	BUSINESS PHONE ( )

MILITARY RANK (IF NOW IN SERVICE)	SEPARATION DATE	UNIT AND DUTY STATION	SOCIAL SECURITY NO.
SOURCE OF OTHER INCOME (Alimony, child support, or separate maintenance need not be revealed if you do not wish to have it considered as a basis for repaying this obligation)	SOURCE	INCOME $	☐ MONTHLY ☐ ANNUALLY

AND YOUR CREDIT REFERENCES ARE

NAME AND ADDRESS OF BANK/SAVINGS AND LOAN	☐ CHECKING ☐ SAVINGS ☐ LOAN	PREVIOUS BELK OR LEGGETT ACCOUNT? ACCOUNT NO. HOW IS ACCOUNT LISTED?	☐ YES ☐ NO

List Bank cards, Dept. Stores, Finance Co.'s, and other accounts:	NAME	ACCOUNT NO.	BALANCE	PAYMENT
			$	$
			$	$
			$	$
			$	$

INFORMATION REGARDING JOINT APPLICANT

COMPLETE THIS AREA IF	☐ JOINT ACCOUNT IS REQUESTED	☐ YOU ARE RELYING ON SPOUSE'S INCOME OR CREDIT HISTORY TO OBTAIN CREDIT

FIRST NAME	MIDDLE INITIAL	LAST NAME	AGE	RELATIONSHIP	SOCIAL SECURITY NO.
JOINT APPLICANT'S ADDRESS IF DIFFERENT FROM APPLICANT ADDRESS	CITY	STATE		ZIP	

JOINT APPLICANT'S PRESENT EMPLOYER	ADDRESS		HOW LONG EMPLOYED YRS. MOS.
BUSINESS PHONE ( )	POSITION/TITLE	MONTHLY INCOME $	

YOUR SIGNATURE PLEASE

Store Stamp Below

I have read and agree to the Terms and Conditions of the Belk Retail Charge Agreement as set forth on attached. Belk is authorized to investigate my credit record and exchange credit experience with other creditors and Credit Reporting Agencies. This information is given to obtain credit, and is true and complete.

FOR OFFICE USE ONLY

Letter ______________

CB. RPT. ______________

EMP. VER ______________

____
Applicant's Signature   Date

DATE	EMP.	#CARDS	T/C	CR/LN.	APPROVED

____
Joint Applicant's signature
(required if joint applicant section completed)   Date

(Continued)

Name____

1. Why might it be important for a creditor to know how long you have lived at your current address?
   (Student response.)

2. What will credit references tell a creditor about you?
   (Student response.)

3. If you were a creditor, would you grant yourself credit? Why or why not?
   (Student response.)

Shopping for Credit

Name ___________________________________

Date _________________________ Period _______________

Shop for a credit card with three different creditors, selecting at least one retailer. Fill in the following chart to help you make comparisons. Then answer the question below.

Credit Source:		(Chart answers are student response.)	
Annual percentage rate			
Other APRs			
Variable-rate information			
Grace period for repayment of balances for purchases			
Method of computing the balance for purchases			
Annual fees			
Minimum finance charge			
Other fees			

Which creditor has the best offer? (Student response.) ____________________________

Explain your answer. (Student response.) _______________________________________

____

____

____

____

____

____

Monthly Credit Statement

Activity E   Name __________________________________

Chapter 9   Date _______________   Period ___________

Refer to the monthly credit statement in 9-8 of the text as you answer the questions below.

1. What is the account number? __5211-7627-58__

2. What is the annual percentage rate charged on the account if the total balance is not paid in full each month? __18 percent__

3. What is the balance remaining at the beginning of the current billing period? __$286.63__

4. What is the total amount of charges made during the billing period? __$428.22__

5. What is the balance remaining at the end of the current billing period? __$457.80__

6. On what date was the statement prepared? __11-28-XX__

7. By what date must you pay the minimum payment, or if you want to avoid finance charges, the new balance? __12-23-XX__

8. What is the minimum payment that must be paid? __$23.00__

9. What is the total amount that can be charged to this account? __$2,000.00__

10. What is the amount of credit available in this account? __$1,542.20__

11. What is the finance charge for this statement? __$7.08__

12. What is the average daily balance? __$471.90__

13. How much was the last payment? __$264.13__

14. How should checks be made out? __Payable to Charge Card__

Consumer Credit Laws

Name _______________________________

Date _______________   Period _______________

Some of the laws that protect you when you use credit are listed below. Indicate, by letter, which law applies to each of the following situations and briefly describe how the law protects you in each case.

A. Truth in Lending Law   E. Fair Debt Collection Practices Act

B. Fair Credit Reporting Act   F. Bankruptcy Act

C. Fair Credit Billing Act   G. Electronic Funds Transfer Act

D. Equal Credit Opportunity Act

Situation:	Law	How It Protects You:
1. A retail store refuses your application for credit with no explanation.	B	(Student response.)
2. Your monthly statement shows no credit and an additional finance charge for an amount you paid.	C	(Student response.)
3. You are behind on car payments. A debt collector has called you at home after 11 p.m. several times.	E	(Student response.)
4. You are borrowing $7,000 to buy a used car. You cannot figure out what the annual percentage rate or dollar cost of finance charges will be.	A	(Student response.)
5. You are refused credit by a bank on the basis of a credit report you think is false.	B	(Student response.)

(Continued)

Name____

6. A debt collector threatens you because you are three months behind on furniture payments.	E	(Student response.)
7. You are billed for merchandise you did not buy.	C	(Student response.)
8. You used credit too freely and then lost your job. Your debts are totally beyond your ability to pay. Your only hope is a fresh start.	F	(Student response.)
9. Your debts are temporarily out of control. You want to pay but need relief and help.	F	(Student response.)
10. You have a good job and you are married. You are refused a credit account in your own name because you have a lower income than your spouse.	D	(Student response.)
11. You lose your ATM card and discover someone has withdrawn $300 from your account.	G	(Student response.)

Chapter 10
Insurance

New Marriage, New Jobs, New Decisions

Activity A

Chapter 10

Name _______________________________

Date _________________ Period _______________

Read the following case study and answer the discussion questions that follow.

> Hector and Jessica are recently married and newly employed. Hector works for a local newspaper and Jessica works in the dean's office of a college.
>
> As new employees, both Hector and Jessica are presented with a package of employee benefits to consider. Hector's company offers health insurance with a choice between an HMO or a PPO. Jessica's company offers health insurance through an HDHP or an HMO. The coverage and cost varies for each type of plan.
>
> Up to this point, Hector and Jessica have been fit and healthy. Most of their previous medical expenses were paid by family insurance policies held by their parents. Hector and Jessica have not thought much about the cost of health care because it has never been a problem for them. However, they plan to take a very close look at the health coverage their employers are offering.

1. If you were in Jessica and Hector's position, what health care benefits would be most important to you? (Student response.)

____

____

____

____

____

____

2. What factors would you consider when choosing among an HMO, an HDHP, or a PPO? _______
(Student response.)

____

____

____

____

(Continued)

Name_______________________________

3. Suppose both Hector and Jessica are offered health protection that covers both spouses. Under what circumstances should they choose individual coverage from their respective employers? When would they be wise to sign up for only one plan? (Student response.)

____

____

____

____

____

____

4. How can an employee decide what, if any, health insurance coverage is needed in addition to employer-provided benefits? (Student response.)

____

____

____

____

____

____

5. What important points should you consider when evaluating group insurance plans? _______
(Student response.)

____

____

____

____

____

Life Insurance

Name ____

Date _________________________ Period ______________________

Demonstrate your understanding of the following insurance coverages and options by briefly describing each of them in your own words.

Coverage/option	Description
Term life	Provides protection only for one, five, ten, or twenty years or until a specified age. When the term ends, so does the protection. May include a renewable option.
Whole life	Provides basic lifetime protection so long as premiums are paid. Face amount is paid to the beneficiaries upon death of the insured. Coverage builds cash value over the years.
Limited payment policy	Offers lifetime protection. Premiums are paid over time, such as 20 years, or until a certain age. Premiums are higher and cash value builds faster than standard whole life coverage.
Variable life	Premiums are fixed and protection is combined with an investment feature. Face value varies with the performance of the investment fund. Guarantees a minimum death benefit.
Adjustable life	Policy can be revised as needs change. Within limits, premiums, face value, and premium payment period may be raised or lowered.

(Continued)

Name ____

Universal life	Permits the adjustment of premiums, face value, and level of protection. Offers an investment feature. Cash value is invested to earn interest at current market rates.
Endowment	Pays the face value of the policy to beneficiaries if the insured dies before the endowment period ends. Pays the face amount to the insured if he or she lives beyond the endowment period.
Group life	Available through employers, unions, or other groups. Costs less than individual policies. The employer or other group may pay all or part of the premium.
Guaranteed renewability	Allows coverage to be kept at the end of a term without new evidence of insurability. Premium rates increase.
Double indemnity	Provides for double benefits if death is the result of an accident.
Disability benefit	Provides for a waiver of premiums if the insured becomes permanently and totally disabled.
Convertible provision	Permits the conversion or exchange of a term policy for another form of protection without new evidence of insurability.

Home Contents Inventory

Name _______________________________________

Date ___________________ Period _______________

Make an inventory of furnishings and possessions in each room of your home. This inventory would assist you in making insurance claims in the event of loss or damage to individual items or a major loss due to fire, etc. When you are finished, file the chart in a safe place.

Attic: (Chart answers are student response.)

Bedroom:

Bedroom:

Living Room:

Family Room/Den:

Basement:

(Continued)

Name_______________________________

Bedroom: (Chart answers are student response.)	Bathrooms:	Closets/Storage Areas:
Dining Room:	**Kitchen:**	**Garage:**

Shopping for Auto Insurance

<table>
<tr><td>Activity D</td><td>Name _______________________________</td></tr>
<tr><td>Chapter 10</td><td>Date ________________ Period ____________</td></tr>
</table>

Shop for the following auto insurance coverages through agents from three different insurance companies to compare costs and services. Complete the chart and answer the questions below.

Types of Coverage	Amounts of Coverage	Annual Premium Charges		
		Company A	Company B	Company C
Bodily injury liability	$300,000/300,000		(Chart answers are student response.)	
Property damage liability	$100,000			
Medical payments/ personal injury protection	$50,000			
Collision	$500 deductible			
Comprehensive physical damage	$1,000 deductible			
Uninsured motorist	$300,000			

1. Which types of coverage would you consider reducing to lower your premiums? State the amounts of coverage you would choose and how much lower your premiums would be. ________
   (Student response.)

   ____

   ____

2. How much would you consider increasing your collision and comprehensive deductibles? State how much these increases would lower your premiums. (Student response.) _______________

   ____

   ____

3. Place a check before all of the following discounts for which you qualify. In the blanks following the discounts, indicate how much they can save you.
   _____ Good driver– (Student response.) _______________________________________

   _____ Good student–____

   _____ Nonsmoker–____

(Continued)

Name ____

_____ Multicar household– ____

_____ Antitheft device– ____

_____ Air bags– ____

_____ Other– ____

4. How do claims handling procedures compare from company to company? (Student response.)

____

____

____

____

____

____

5. What additional services does each company offer that are important to you? (Student response.)

____

____

____

____

____

____

6. Choose an insurance carrier and give reasons for your choice. (Student response.)

____

____

____

____

____

____

Your Saver Profile

Activity A

Chapter 11

Name ____

Date _____________________ Period _______________

Use the following questions to determine your profile as a saver.

1. How much money can you save regularly each week? (Student response.) _________________

2. When and how often would you want to deposit money in a savings account? _________________
   (Student response.)

   ____

   ____

3. When and how often would you want to withdraw money from a savings account? _____________
   (Student response.)

   ____

   ____

   ____

4. Would you want an automatic monthly transfer of cash from your checking to your savings account? Explain. (Student response.) _______________________________

   ____

   ____

   ____

   ____

5. Which of the following is most important to you for your savings? (Rank in order of importance).

   ______ Availability of cash as you need it.

   ______ Highest earnings possible.

   ______ Being able to deposit any amount at any time.

   ______ Flexibility in depositing and withdrawing cash without loss of interest.

   ______ Restrictions on withdrawals to encourage savings accumulation.

(Continued)

Name ____

6. Describe your savings goals in terms of:
   Amounts you have to save. (Student response.) ______________________

   ____

   ____

   ____

   ____

   Dates by which you want to save specific amounts. (Student response.) ______

   ____

   ____

   ____

   ____

   Purposes for which you are saving. (Student response.) ______________

   ____

   ____

   ____

   ____

7. Why is it important to have an emergency fund? Explain. (Student response.) ______

   ____

   ____

   ____

   ____

8. Do you think saving money is important? Explain. (Student response.) ______

   ____

   ____

   ____

   ____

Calculating Compound Interest

Name _______________________________

Date _______________ Period _______________

Calculate compound interest earnings for the following situations. Show your work in the space provided.

1. Jacob opens an online-only savings account and deposits $50 each month. The annual interest rate is 2.5 percent. Interest is compounded monthly. What is the total amount in the account after 5 months? $251.56

Month	Step 1	Step 2	Step 3
1	$50 × 2.5% = $1.25	$1.25 ÷ 12 = $0.10	$50 + $0.10 = $50.10
2	$100.10 × 2.5% = $2.50	$2.50 ÷ 12 = $0.21	$100.10 + $0.21 = $100.31
3	$150.31 × 2.5% = $3.76	$3.76 ÷ 12 = $0.31	$150.31 + $0.31 = $150.62
4	$200.62 × 2.5% = $5.02	$5.02 ÷ 12 = $0.42	$200.62 + $0.42 = $201.04
5	$251.04 × 2.5% = $6.28	$6.28 ÷ 12 = $0.52	$251.04 + $0.52 = $251.56

2. Latoya opens a savings account and deposits $1,525. The interest rate is 2.73 percent. Interest is compounded quarterly. How much interest will her deposit earn in one year? _______________
   $42.06 ($1,567.06 − $1,525)

Quarter	Step 1	Step 2	Step 3
1	$1,525 × 2.73% = $41.63	$41.63 ÷ 4 = $10.41	$1,525 + $10.41 = $1,535.41
2	$1,535.41 × 2.73% = $41.92	$41.92 ÷ 4 = $10.48	$1,535.41 + $10.48 = $1,545.89
3	$1,545.89 × 2.73% = 42.20	$42.20 ÷ 4 = $10.55	$1,545.89 + $42.20 = $1,556.44
4	$1,556.44 × 2.73% = $42.49	$42.49 ÷ 4 = $10.62	$1,556.44 + 10.62 = $1,567.06

Your Savings Program

Name ____

Date _________________   Period _______________

Compare two savings choices offered by a financial institution. Then choose the savings method best for you and answer the following questions. (Answers are student response.)

1. Purposes for which I am saving: ____

   ____

2. Amount to be saved: $__________________ by (date)___________________________________

3. Amount of cash available for an initial deposit: $ _______________________________________

4. Amount of cash available for regular weekly or monthly deposits: $__________ per____________

5. Name of financial institution: ____

6. Are the deposits of this financial institution insured?____________________________________

7. In a regular savings account, money market deposit account, or online-only savings account:

   Rate of interest paid: ____

   Method of calculating interest:____

   Frequency of compounding interest:____

   Interest periods or frequency of crediting interest to the account (monthly, quarterly, semiannually, or annually): ____

   Minimum deposit, if applicable: ____

   Restrictions on making deposits and withdrawals: _______________________________________

8. In a certificate of deposit:

   Annual percentage yield: ____

   Minimum initial deposit: ____

   Maturity or length of time money must remain on deposit:_________________________________

   Penalties for early withdrawals:____

   Options for reinvestment at maturity:____

9. Which savings program is most appropriate for you? Explain your decision.___________________
   (Student response.)

   ____

   ____

   ____

   ____

   ____

Chapter 12
Investing and Estate Planning

Evaluating Stocks

Activity A

Chapter 12

Name _______________________________________

Date __________________ Period __________________

Select three companies listed on the New York Stock Exchange. Using library resources, newspapers, stockbrokers, Web sites, and annual reports as sources of information, fill in the chart below. Then answer the following question.

Information	Companies:		
	1.	**2.**	**3.**
Type of business or industry		(Chart answers are student response.)	
Industry outlook			
Current price per share			
Highest price per share over the past year			
Lowest price per share over the past year			
Price/ earnings ratio			
Dividends paid per share over the past year			
Earnings per share last year			

If you were planning to make an investment in stocks, which company would you choose? Explain your answer. (Student response.) ____

____

____

____

Mutual Funds and Money Market Funds

Name _________________________________

Date _________________ Period _____________

Obtain a prospectus or descriptive folder on a specific fund from a broker or fund manager or online. Fill in the following information about the fund. (Answers are student response.)

Name of fund: _________________ Company: _________________________________

Key objectives of the fund: ____

____

Type of fund:____

Mix of investments in the fund: ____

Net asset value $_________________

How would you rate the experience and qualifications of those who manage the fund? ___________

____

What is the investment record of the fund over the last five years? ____________________

____

What are some securities the fund holds? ______________________________________

____

What are the investment policies? ____

____

____

How often are dividends declared?____

How are dividends distributed—cash, new shares, your option? ______________________

____

Will you pay a commission to buy shares in the fund? _________ If so, how much?_____________

Will you have to pay a fee to sell? _________ If so, how much?______________________

Comments:____

____

____

____

____

____

Last Will and Testament

Activity C

Chapter 12

Name _________________________________

Date _______________ Period _______________

In the space provided, write a brief paragraph on each of the following topics. You can obtain the information you need from books on estate planning, articles on financial magazines or newspapers, state and national bar associations, interviews with attorneys, and by searching the Internet.

Your state's laws governing the distribution of assets in an estate when there is no will. _____________
(Student response.)

____

____

____

____

____

____

Provisions to include in a will. (Student response.) ______________________________

____

____

____

____

____

____

Consequences of dying without a legal will. (Student response.) ________________

____

____

____

____

____

Estate Planning Match-Up

Name ___________________________

Date _______________   Period _______________

Match the following words and phrases related to estate planning to their meanings.

___J___ 1. A legal document stating what is to be done with a person's estate at his or her death.

___E___ 2. A person named to take responsibility of any beneficiaries who are young children.

___I___ 3. A person or institution named to manage assets on behalf of the beneficiaries.

___F___ 4. A statement of instructions for specific medical treatment if a person becomes unable to make medical decisions.

___C___ 5. A person appointed to carry out the terms of a will.

___H___ 6. A legal document that gives a trustee the authority to manage the assets in an estate on behalf of the beneficiaries.

___A___ 7. An amendment added when minor changes are made to a signed will.

___G___ 8. The government institution that makes decisions about a deceased individual's will and estate.

___B___ 9. The assets and liabilities a person leaves when he or she dies.

___D___ 10. A person who has transferred his or her assets to a trust.

A. codicil

B. estate

C. executor

D. grantor

E. guardian

F. living will

G. probate court

H. trust

I. trustee

J. will

Chapter 13
Smart Shopping Basics
Rating the Sellers

Activity A

Chapter 13

Name _______________________________

Date _________________ Period _______________

Select an item you would like to buy such as a camera, cellular phone, game system, or bicycle. Shop for the item from four different sellers. Include at least one online seller. Using the form below, rate the characteristics of each seller as follows:

Excellent 4

Good 3

Fair 2

Poor 1

Unacceptable 0

Item: _______________________________

Seller Characteristics	Seller 1	Seller 2	Seller 3	Seller 4
Wide selection of item you want		(Chart answers are student response.)		
Helpful salespeople (or description in catalog or on Web site)				
Competitive prices				
Consumer services you want (deliveries, special orders, etc.)				
Atmosphere you like				
Reasonable policies on returns, exchanges, refunds, etc.				
Other characteristics important to you				
Total score				

From which seller would you purchase this item? Explain why. (Student response.) _______________________

____

____

Rating Product Tests

Name _______________________________

Date ________________   Period _______________

Select an item that you want to buy. Check its rating with two consumer ratings services. Then answer the following questions about the testing and rating information.

Item: ____

Evaluation Questions	Consumer Ratings Service #1:	Consumer Ratings Service #2:
Who sponsored or conducted the testing?	(Chart answers are student response.)	
What features and performance standards were tested?		
What test methods were used?		
Under what conditions were the tests conducted?		
What do the test results mean to you?		
What factors are important to you that were not included in testing?		

Shopping Courtesy

Activity C

Chapter 13

Name _______________________________

Date _______________ Period _______________

Visit a store of your choice. Observe shoppers and salespeople for 15 to 30 minutes. Look for examples of courtesy and rudeness on the part of salespeople and consumers. Write a brief description of an example of courtesy and of rudeness. Discuss your examples in class.

Example of courtesy:

(Student response.)

____

____

____

____

____

____

____

____

Example of rudeness:

(Student response.)

____

____

____

____

____

____

____

____

____

Shopping for Services

Name _________________________________

Date _________________ Period _________________

Interview a person who provides a service, such as a physician, auto mechanic, lawyer, or beautician. Ask the following questions:

1. What services do you provide for consumers? (Student response.) _______________________

____

____

2. How much do your services cost? (Student response.) _______________________

____

3. What does the price of the service include? (Student response.) _______________________

____

4. What do you expect of consumers? (Student response.) _______________________

____

5. How would you describe an inconsiderate consumer? (Student response.) _______________________

____

6. How can consumers make the most of the services that you provide? (Student response.) _______________________

____

____

Other questions and comments: (Student response.) _______________________

____

____

____

____

____

Chapter 14
Consumers in the Marketplace

Advertising Techniques

Activity A

Chapter 14

Name ___________________________

Date ________________ Period ___________________

List the type of advertising technique used in each of the following examples.

bandwagon	insecurity appeal	statistic
celebrity endorsement	nostalgia	testimonial
green ad	puffery	
humor	sex appeal	

__green ad__________ 1. "Brand X shampoo is made of pure and natural ingredients."

__bandwagon__________ 2. "Everyone is using Brand X cell phone service, and you should too."

__humor__________ 3. In an ad for Brand X dairy products, cows wearing sunglasses and bathing suits sip chocolate milk drinks on a beach. "Mooooore Brand X please," one says.

__insecurity appeal__________ 4. "If your breath smelled fresher, you'd be more popular. Brand X chewing gum can help."

__puffery__________ 5. "Brand X makes the tastiest fried chicken in the entire world."

__testimonial__________ 6. "I'm a busy parent with little time for cleaning up messes. That's why I use Brand X paper towels."

__statistics__________ 7. "Fifty to eighty percent of foodborne illnesses are caused by germs in the home. Protect your family by using Brand X antibacterial kitchen cleaner."

__sex appeal__________ 8. In an ad for lawn mowers, an attractive woman in a bathing suit pushes a Brand X mower across a field.

__celebrity endorsement__________ 9. "I'm a famous actor and I use a Brand X credit card. You should too."

__nostalgia__________ 10. "When I was growing up, my mom made Brand X cocoa to warm me up on wintry afternoons. I make it for my kids today."

Selling Methods

Name _______________________________

Date ____________________ Period _______________

In the space provided, list ways consumers can take advantage of the selling methods businesses use to entice them to buy.

Selling Methods	Advantages to the Consumer
Advertising	(Answers should discuss how advertising can provide some factual product information.)
Special sales and promotions	(Answers should discuss how consumers benefit when they buy items they need on sale.)
Buying incentives	(Answers should discuss how consumers benefit as long as they limit purchases to goods or services they would normally buy or try.)
Packaging and display	(Answers should discuss how packaging can list factual information, convenience features, and ecological claims.)

Consumer Complaints

Activity C

Name ___________________________

Chapter 14

Date _________________ Period ___________

Write a complaint letter or send an e-mail about a consumer problem you have had with a product or service. You may choose instead to write a complaint letter, making up the details, for one of the following problems: (A) a rude salesperson in a department store; (B) a missing part in a packaged product to be assembled by the purchaser; (C) an error in billing charges; (D) a product that fails to perform as advertised and expected; (E) a garment that has been damaged by the cleaners; (F) a cosmetic that has caused a serious allergic reaction.

Use the information given in the text as a guide in preparing your letter.

(Letters are student response, but should follow the format of Figure 14-6.)

Consumer Responsibilities

Name ______________________________

Date ______________   Period ______________

As a consumer, you have rights in the marketplace. However, you also have responsibilities. Eight consumer rights and responsibilities are listed below. On the blank before each responsibility, write the letter of the right that is associated with it.

A. right to safety

B. right to be informed

C. right to choose

D. right to be heard

E. right to satisfaction of basic needs

F. right to redress

G. right to education

H. right to a healthful environment

Consumer Responsibilities

___G___ 1. Take a consumer education or personal finance course.

___E___ 2. Put essential needs ahead of other items when spending. Get the training and education necessary to earn a living wage.

___B___ 3. Find information on products, services, and sellers. Investigate a seller's reputation for honesty and fairness.

___H___ 4. Practice safe and responsible waste disposal and resource conservation.

___D___ 5. Express concerns to appropriate business and government representatives.

___A___ 6. Read and follow product directions regarding use, storage, and disposal.

___F___ 7. Complain effectively to settle disputes with sellers in cases of poor service, shoddy products, or misleading claims.

___C___ 8. Carefully select products and services that best meet needs at affordable prices.

Chapter 15
Spending for Food

Nutrients You Need

Activity A

Chapter 15

Name _______________________________

Date ________________ Period _______________

The following statements describe nutrients listed in Chart 15-1 in the text. Fill in each blank with the appropriate nutrient and answer the questions that follow.

__fat__ 1. Butter, margarine, chocolate, bacon, salad oils, and dressings provide this nutrient.

__iron__ 2. Combines with protein to make hemoglobin.

__thiamin__ 3. Fish, pork, dried beans, and brewer's yeast are sources of this nutrient.

__vitamin A__ 4. Helps keep skin clear and mucous membranes healthy.

__calcium__ 5. Helps build bones and teeth and helps muscles and nerves function properly.

__water__ 6. Helps carry waste products from cells and control body temperature.

__riboflavin__ 7. Helps cells use oxygen and helps keep skin, tongue, and lips normal.

__vitamin C__ 8. Helps wounds heal and broken bones mend and helps the body fight infection.

__vitamin D__ 9. Maintains bone density and helps build strong bones and teeth.

__niacin__ 10. Meat, fish, poultry, milk, peanut butter, and dried beans and peas are sources of this nutrient.

__protein__ 11. Regulates fluid balance in the cells and functions to build and repair tissues.

__vitamin E__ 12. Sources include liver and other variety meats, eggs, leafy green vegetables, and salad oils.

__phosphorus__ 13. Sources include protein and calcium food sources.

(Continued)

Name _______________________________________

___carbohydrate___________ 14. Supplies energy and provides bulk and fiber in the form of cellulose.

___vitamin K_____________ 15. Vitamin that helps blood clot.

Record all the foods you eat for two days.

Day 1	Day 2
(Answers are student response.)	

Does your list include food sources of all six nutrients? (Student response.) ______________

____

List the nutrients, if any that are lacking from your diet. (Student response.) ____________

____

____

____

Why does your body need these nutrients? (Student response.) ___________________

____

____

____

____

Which foods could you add to your diet to obtain these nutrients? (Student response.) ______

____

____

____

____

Planning with MyPyramid

Name ___________________________________

Date _________________ Period _______________

List six of your favorite foods. In the space provided, plan a healthful menu around each food.
Include foods from all groups in MyPyramid in each menu.

1. Favorite food: _(Student response.)_______________________________

   Menu:

2. Favorite food: _(Student response.)_______________________________

   Menu:

3. Favorite food: _(Student response.)_______________________________

   Menu:

(Continued)

Name____

4. Favorite food: (Student response.)__________________________________

    Menu:

5. Favorite food: (Student response.)__________________________________

    Menu:

6. Favorite food: (Student response.)__________________________________

    Menu:

Food Prices

Activity C

Chapter 15

Name _______________________________

Date _________________ Period _______________

Make a shopping list of at least 12 items your family buys regularly at the grocery store. Estimate the price of each item. Then check the price at the store where your family shops most frequently and enter the actual cost of the item. List the difference between the estimated price and the actual cost for each item. Then answer the questions below.

Grocery List	Estimated Price	Actual Cost	Cost Difference
(Answers are student response.)			

How many items did you estimate within 10 cents of the actual cost? (Student response.)

Which items were more expensive than your estimates? (Student response.)

Which items were less expensive than your estimates? (Student response.)

What were your biggest surprises? (Student response.)

Choosing Where to Buy Food

Activity D   Name ____

Chapter 15   Date ________________   Period _______________

Visit a grocery store of your choice and answer the following questions.

1. How do regular food prices and specials compare with the prices and specials at other food stores?
   (Student response.) ____

   ____

2. Are fresh foods, such as dairy products, meats, fish, poultry, produce, bakery products, and deli foods, delivered or prepared daily? (Student response.) Do they appear fresh, clean, and wholesome? (Student response.) ____________________

3. Is the frozen food kept well below freezing? (Student response.) ____________

4. Does the selection of foods and groceries suit your needs and preferences? Explain.
   (Student response.) ____

   ____

5. Is it easy to find the foods that you want? (Student response.) ______________

6. Does the food store contain a: _____ delicatessen, _____ bakery, _____ pharmacy, _____ newsstand, _____ ATM? Which of these are most important to you? Explain.
   (Student response.) ____

   ____

7. Are the store employees generally helpful, knowledgeable, and pleasant? (Student response.) ____

8. Does the store offer: _____ check cashing, _____ coupon exchanges, _____ unit pricing, _____ open dating, _____ nutrition information, or _____ express checkout? (Student response.)

9. Does the store follow fair policies, such as honest advertising, rain checks for specials that run out, or replacements or refunds for purchases that are not satisfactory? (Student response.) ____

10. Is the store clean, attractive, and well-maintained? (Student response.) __________

11. Is the store in a convenient location for you? (Student response.) ______________

12. Is the store open during the hours you want to shop? (Student response.) __________

13. Is the overall atmosphere of the store acceptable to you? Explain. (Student response.) ______

14. Explain why you would or would not shop regularly in this store.
    (Student response.) ____

    ____

    ____

Consumer Food-Buying Tips

Activity E

Chapter 15

Name ______________________________

Date __________________ Period ______________________

Pretend you are writing a consumer column for a newspaper, magazine, or Web site. Next to each of the following foods, list tips to use when buying these foods. On a separate sheet of paper, write an article featuring food buying tips for consumers.

Foods	Buying Tips
Dairy foods	Buy fresh products in the form needed; buy low-fat varieties.
Eggs	Select eggs with clean, uncracked shells.
Meat	Look for government inspection and grading; choose firm, well-marbled meat; compare meat cuts and prices; consider variety meats.
Poultry	Choose clean, moist, plump birds with meaty breasts, legs, and thighs. Buy whole chickens, which are less expensive than cut pieces. Chicken with the bone in is less expensive than boneless. Buy young or mature chicken depending on your recipe.
Fish and shellfish	Look for firm flesh; tight, shiny scales; bright, bulging eyes; and no smell.
Fruits and vegetables	Buy fresh produce in season. Consider size, weight, freshness, ripeness, and appearance. Canned or frozen fruits and vegetables that are chopped, sliced, or cut cost less than whole pieces.
Grain products	Ready-to-serve products generally cost more than home baked or those requiring some preparation. Special rice products tend to cost more than white rice that requires cooking.

Eating Out

Name _______________________________________

Date ____________________   Period _______________

Visit, phone, or look up Web sites for two local restaurants. Complete the following information about each restaurant. (You may wish to expand on this activity. Prepare a guide of local restaurants by filling out an information card for each restaurant in your area.)

Restaurant name _(Answers are student response.)_______________________

Address____ Telephone_________________

Type of food served:____

Price range: (Check one.) _____ Expensive _____ Inexpensive _____ In-between

Hours of food service:____

Reservations: (Check one.) _____ Required _____ Accepted _____ Not accepted _____ Not needed

Atmosphere: (Check one.) _____ Casual _____ Formal _____ In-between

_____ Other—Describe: ____

Dress code: (Check one.) _____ Coat and tie _____ Casual _____ None stated

_____ Other—Describe: ____

Comments:____

____

____

Restaurant name ____

Address____ Telephone_________________

Type of food served:____

Price range: (Check one.) _____ Expensive _____ Inexpensive _____ In-between

Hours of food service:____

Reservations: (Check one.) _____ Required _____ Accepted _____ Not accepted _____ Not needed

Atmosphere: (Check one.) _____ Casual _____ Formal _____ In-between

_____ Other—Describe: ____

Dress code: (Check one.) _____ Coat and tie _____ Casual _____ None stated

_____ Other—Describe: ____

Comments:____

In the space below, describe your favorite restaurant._______________________

____

____

Chapter 16
Clothing

Clothes, Feelings, and Behavior

Activity A
Chapter 16

Name _______________________________________

Date ___________________ Period ________________

Complete the following sentences.

1. When my clothes are different from everyone else's at a party or at school, it makes me feel ______
   (Student response.) ____

2. The main difference between being dressed up and casual is (Student response.) ______________
   ____

3. My idea of being well-dressed is (Student response.) ____________________________
   ____

4. My favorite outfit to wear is (Student response.) ________________________________
   ____

5. When I wear a new outfit for the first time, I feel (Student response.) ________________
   ____

6. When I wear old, sloppy clothes, I feel (Student response.) ____________________
   ____

7. Being dressed up makes me feel (Student response.) ____________________________
   ____

8. The most treasured item in my wardrobe is (Student response.) ____________ because
   ____

9. When I want to put my best foot forward, I wear (Student response.) ______________
   ____

10. My three greatest clothing mistakes were (Student response.) ________________
    ____

11. The thing I notice first in the way other people look is (Student response.) __________
    ____

12. Clothes can affect the way I feel and act because (Student response.) ______________
    ____

The Smart Shopper Quiz

Name _______________________________

Date ______________________ Period _______________

Answer yes or no to the following questions.   (Answers are student response.)

_______ 1. Do you set up a clothing budget and plan purchases in advance each season?

_______ 2. Do you research fashions, fabrics, and stores before buying clothes?

_______ 3. Do you know the basic steps to follow when you have a complaint about clothing durability, performance, or care?

_______ 4. Do you know at least five quality and construction features to look for in different types of clothing?

_______ 5. Do you know some of the basic characteristics and common uses of different fibers and fabrics?

_______ 6. Do you inspect garments carefully before buying?

_______ 7. Do you check fit and appearance in a full-length mirror before buying?

_______ 8. Do you read labels to learn about fiber content and care requirements?

_______ 9. Are you firm with pushy salespeople, not letting them pressure you into purchases that are not right for you?

_______ 10. Do you understand common terms used to describe fashions, styles, fabrics, finishes, colors, and care recommendations?

_______ 11. Do you know your most flattering colors and styles?

_______ 12. Do you plan new purchases to coordinate with clothes and accessories you already own?

_______ 13. Do you know which stores in your area are most likely to carry clothing and accessories you want?

_______ 14. Are you familiar with policies regarding returns, exchanges, and charges in stores where you shop?

_______ 15. Are you generally satisfied with most of your clothing purchases?

Scoring: Give yourself 10 points for each honest yes. If your score is less than 100, you need to sharpen your clothing shopping skills.

Complete this statement:

My score of _______ reflects _(Student response.)_____________________________________

____

I could improve my clothing shopping skills by _(Student response.)___________________

____

____

____

My Wardrobe Inventory

<table>
<tr><td>Activity C</td><td>Name ___________________________________</td></tr>
<tr><td>Chapter 16</td><td>Date _________________ Period _______________</td></tr>
</table>

Use the chart below to make an inventory of all the clothes, shoes, and accessories that you own and need.

Clothes for:	Have – Description	Need – Description	Estimated Cost
SCHOOL sweaters shirts pants skirts		(Chart answers are student response.)	
AT HOME old clothes casuals sleepwear sweats			
WORK uniforms clothes for job			
DRESS suits dresses shirts			
SPORTS team wear swimsuits tennis ski wear			
FOOTWEAR shoes boots			
OUTERWEAR coats jackets hats/gloves/ scarves			
EXTRAS jewelry ties			

(Continued)

Name _______________________________________

1. List items that you no longer wear, need, or want. (Student response.)

   ____

   ____

   ____

   ____

2. List places where you could sell, trade, or dispose of the items listed above. (Student response.)

   ____

   ____

   ____

   ____

3. What is the total cost of the items you listed as *needs*? (Student response.)

   ____

Clothing Characteristics

Name _______________________________

Date _______________   Period _______________

In the space provided, rank the following clothing characteristics in the order of their importance to you from the most to least important. Then sketch a picture or mount a picture from a magazine that illustrates the characteristic(s) you consider most important.

Attractive	Practical	Same as friends wear
Comfortable	Colorful	Easy care
Fashionable	Functional	Desirable brand name
Economical	Different	Good line and design

1. (Answers are student response.)
2. _______________________
3. _______________________
4. _______________________

5. _______________________
6. _______________________
7. _______________________
8. _______________________

9. _______________________
10. _______________________
11. _______________________
12. _______________________

Illustration:

Characteristic(s) illustrated: (Student response.) _______________________

____

____

____

Caring for Clothes

Activity E

Chapter 16

Name _______________________________________

Date _____________________ Period __________________

In the space provided, copy the information found on the fiber content and care labels of two of your favorite garments. Use information from the labels to answer the questions that follow.

<table>
<tr><td>Fiber Content Label #1</td><td>Clothing Care Label #1</td></tr>
</table>

1. Describe the type of garment from which these labels came. (Student response.) ____________

2. Is this garment made from a fiber blend? __________ If so, what fibers are used and what are the advantages of combining them? (Student response.) ___________________________________

   ____

   If the garment is made from a single fiber, what are the advantages and disadvantages of this fiber? (Student response.) ____

   ____

3. Who manufactured this garment? (Student response.) ___________________________________

4. Was this garment imported? __________ If so, from what country? (Student response.) ________

5. Explain what is meant by the care instructions given on the care label. (Student response.) ______

   ____

   ____

6. What type of routine care does this garment need to keep it in good condition? ________________
   (Student response.)

   ____

   ____

7. How should this garment be stored? (Student response.) _________________________________

   ____

Chapter 17
Health and Wellness

Personal Care Product Inventory

Activity A

Chapter 17

Name _______________________________________

Date ____________________ Period _______________

Use the chart below to take inventory of your personal care products.

Product	Brand Name	Price	Effectiveness
For the hair Shampoo Conditioner Hair spray Mousse Other: ____________	(Chart answers are student response.)		
For the face Cleanser Soap Acne treatment Shaving cream or gel Moisturizer Foundation/Powder Blusher Lipstick Other: ____________			
For the eyes Eye drops Eyeliner Eye shadow Mascara Eyebrow pencil Eye makeup remover Other: ____________			
		Subtotal:	

(Continued)

Name ____

For the mouth Toothpaste Dental floss Mouthwash Other: ___________			
For the hands Hand lotion Cuticle remover Nail polish Nail polish remover Other: ___________			
For the body Soap Body wash Lotion Powder Deodorant Cologne Sunscreen Other: ___________			

Total: ________

Total the price column to see how much you are spending on personal care products.______________
(Student response.) ____

Do you feel you are getting your money's worth? (Student response.) _______________________
____

What are some ways to maximize your dollars when buying personal care products?______________
(Student response.) ____

____

What new products or brands would you like to try? (Student response.) _____________________

____

What grooming services are part of your personal care routine? (Student response.) ___________

____

____

How much do you usually spend on grooming services? (Student response.) __________________

____

Health Care Specialists

Name _______________________________

Date _________________   Period _______________

Match each specialist listed below with the correct description.

__L__ 1. Treats diseases and disorders of the ear, nose, and throat.

__B__ 2. Treats diseases of the skin, hair, and nails.

__E__ 3. Treats disorders of the brain, spinal cord, and nervous system.

__H__ 4. Diagnoses and treats abnormalities of the eyes.

__K__ 5. Treats fractures, deformities, and diseases of bones, joints, and skeletal system.

__P__ 6. Deals with the urinary tract and male reproductive system.

__O__ 7. Performs operations to diagnose or treat a variety of diseases or physical conditions.

__D__ 8. Provides a broad range of health care services; diagnoses and treats physical diseases.

__C__ 9. Diagnoses and treats disorders affecting women, particularly those relating to reproductive organs.

__A__ 10. Diagnoses and treats diseases and disorders of the heart.

__M__ 11. Deals with the development and care of infants, children, and adolescents.

__F__ 12. Provides medical care for women during pregnancy and childbirth.

__J__ 13. Corrects irregularities and deformities of the teeth, usually with braces.

__I__ 14. Performs operations to extract teeth and to treat injuries and defects of the jaw and mouth.

__G__ 15. Diagnoses and treats tumors.

__N__ 16. Diagnoses and treats mental and emotional disorders.

A. Cardiologist	I. Oral surgeon
B. Dermatologist	J. Orthodontist
C. Gynecologist	K. Orthopedist
D. Internist	L. Otolaryngologist
E. Neurologist	M. Pediatrician
F. Obstetrician	N. Psychiatrist
G. Oncologist	O. Surgeon
H. Ophthalmologist	P. Urologist

Having Fun

Name _______________________________

Date _________________ Period _______________

Complete the following sentences.

1. Three things I really like to do for fun are <u>(Student response.)</u>

____

____

____

2. If I had \$25 to spend on a leisure activity, I would <u>(Student response.)</u>

____

____

3. If I had \$150 to spend on sports or hobby equipment, I would buy <u>(Student response.)</u>

____

____

____

4. If I had \$500 to spend on vacation and travel, I would <u>(Student response.)</u>

____

____

____

5. Three things I really like to do but never have enough money for are <u>(Student response.)</u>

____

____

____

6. Three free or low-cost activities available in my community are <u>(Student response.)</u>

____

____

____

7. Three ways I could stretch the money I spend for fun are <u>(Student response.)</u>

____

____

____

Chapter 18
Housing

Housing Choices

Activity A

Chapter 18

Name ____

Date ___________________ Period _______________

In the space below, describe what you believe to be the pros and cons of the housing choices presented. Then make your choices and give reasons for them.

	City	vs.	Suburb
Pros	(Answers are student response.)		Pros
Cons			Cons

	New	vs.	Older
Pros			Pros
Cons			Cons

(Continued)

Name____

	Apartment	**vs.**	**House**	

Pros | | **Pros**

Cons | | **Cons**

	Rent	**vs.**	**Own**	

Pros | | **Pros**

Cons | | **Cons**

In the space provided, check your housing preferences and list the reasons for your choices.

Choices	**Reasons**
_____ City _____ Suburb	(Student response.)
_____ New _____ Older	(Student response.)
_____ Apartment _____ House	(Student response.)
_____ Rent _____ Own	(Student response.)

How Much Can They Afford?

Name ____

Date ___________________   Period _______________

Practice using the two formulas to estimate how much money could be budgeted for housing in the following situations.

FORMULA 1 (for use with situations 1, 2, and 3): Budget one-third of the net monthly income for housing costs.

1. Hayley's net monthly income is $1,900. She and a friend found an apartment to rent for $1,000 a month, including utilities. If Hayley and her friend split the rent, can she afford this apartment? _Yes__ What is the maximum amount this formula allows Hayley for housing? $633______

2. Maurice has a net monthly income of $2,400. He has found an apartment he likes that rents for $750 a month. All utilities are included in his rent. Can Maurice afford this apartment? _Yes__ What is the maximum amount he could budget for rent? $800______

3. Justin and Ivy Harboski have a joint net monthly income of $2,750. They have figured their monthly mortgage payments for the house they want to buy would be $1,025. Can they afford to buy the house? _No.______ Why or why not?__This formula only allows $917 per month for a_____ mortgage.

____

____

FORMULA 2 (for use with situations 4, 5, and 6): Budget no more than two and one-half times the gross annual income for the purchase price of a dwelling.

4. Shelli and Alyssa would like to pool their resources and buy a house. Each has a gross annual income of $23,500. How much can they each afford to spend? What is the maximum price they should consider when looking for a house? $58,750, $117,500

____

5. Richard's gross annual income is $41,000. How much can he afford to spend if he decides he wants to buy a condominium? $102,500

____

6. Bill and Mary Smith have a combined gross annual income of $75,000. How much can they afford to spend for the purchase of a home? $187,500

____

Shopping for Furniture

Activity C

Chapter 18

Name _______________________________

Date ____________________ Period ____________________

Choose a major furniture item or grouping such as a sofa, bedroom set, desk, lounge chair, or dining room set. Shop for it in at least three outlets. Use the following checklist where the questions apply. Then answer the question at the end.

Furniture item or grouping: (Answers are student response.) _______________________________

Outlet #1: ____________________   Outlet #2: ____________________   Outlet #3: ____________________

(Chart answers are student response.)

	Outlet #1		Outlet #2		Outlet #3	
	Yes	No	Yes	No	Yes	No
Will the furniture be useful at the end of five years?						
Is it made of appropriate, quality materials inside and out?						
Is it made well?						
Will it wear well?						
Are clear care instructions given?						
Is the color, size, and design right for your space and needs?						
Is the price reasonable?						
Are delivery, assembly, and installation services available?						
Are the charges for these services fair?						
Does the manufacturer have a good name and reputation?						
Is the seller reputable and honest?						
Does the seller seem concerned with your needs?						
Can you return the item?						
Does it carry a warranty?						
Can it be delivered in a reasonable length of time?						

(Continued)

Name_______________________________

Additional questions if you are shopping for case goods:

(Chart answers are student response.)

	Outlet #1		Outlet #2		Outlet #3	
	Yes	No	Yes	No	Yes	No
Do doors shut tightly without sticking?						
Are doors held shut with magnetic catches?						
Are drawers and doors flush with openings?						
Have comer blocks been used for reinforcement?						
Has dovetail construction been used on drawers?						
Are there dust panels between drawers?						
Do drawers slide easily?						
Are legs attached with mortise and tenon or dowel joints?						
Do legs stand squarely on the floor?						
Are insides, backsides, and undersides sanded and finished?						
Is hardware attractive and securely attached?						
Will surfaces stand the wear you will give them?						

Additional questions if shopping for sleep furniture:

	Outlet #1		Outlet #2		Outlet #3	
	Yes	No	Yes	No	Yes	No
Is mattress resilient and comfortable?						
Is edge of bed firm when you sit on it?						
Is mattress odor free?						
Does bed frame have casters or rollers for easy moving?						
Do mattress and springs go together?						
Does mattress have strong handles attached for easy handling and turning?						
Is mattress cover strong and closely woven with vents on each side?						
Does the price include mattress, springs, and frame?						
Does cross-sectional sample of mattress show quality construction?						
Is mattress treated to resist soil, stain, and mildew?						
Is mattress nonflammable?						

 (Continued)

Name____

Additional questions if shopping for upholstered furniture:

(Chart answers are student response.)	Outlet #1		Outlet #2		Outlet #3	
	Yes	No	Yes	No	Yes	No
Are legs and joints securely attached?						
Do you know what type of springs are used and how they are attached?						
Do you know facts on cushion materials and construction?						
Do cushions have zipper closings?						
Are cushions reversible?						
Is outer covering well tailored?						
Will upholstery fabric wear well?						
Is there a soil or stain resistant finish?						
Is the furniture comfortable?						
Are patterned fabrics well matched?						

From which outlet would you purchase this furniture item or grouping? (Student response.)

Explain why. (Student response.)

____

____

____

____

____

____

____

____

____

____

____

____

____

Financing a Home

Name ______________________________________

Date ___________________ Period ______________

Assume that you are buying a home and need financing. The following options are available. Give a brief description along with the advantages and disadvantages of each.

Description	Advantages	Disadvantages
Fixed rate mortgage: Guarantees a fixed or unchanging interest rate for the life of the loan.	Loan rate does not go up or down as the economy changes.	Even if interest rates drop after the loan is written, the loan keeps its initial rate. To get a lower rate, the borrower must go through a time-consuming and costly process of refinancing.
Adjustable rate mortgage: Interest rate is adjusted up or down periodically.	Often offered at lower interest rates than fixed rate mortgages.	Risk of increased interest rates and loan payments when adjustments are made.
Graduated payment mortgage: Allows the buyer to pay low monthly payments at first and higher payments in the future.	Low monthly payments in the early years of the loan.	Risk of being unable to make higher payments if earnings do not increase.
Interest only mortgage: Monthly payments are applied only to the interest, not the principal, for a certain number of years.	Low monthly payments for a certain period of time.	After the specified number of years, the borrower must begin making higher payments, pay off the loan, or renegotiate a new mortgage at prevailing rates and terms.

(Continued)

Name ____

Description	Advantages	Disadvantages
Subprime mortgage: Made by lenders who charge higher than prime rates to borrowers who have poor or no credit ratings.	Borrowers who have poor or no credit ratings and who often do not qualify for mortgages from other lenders can obtain these loans.	Charge substantially higher interest than prime rates.
First-time homebuyer program: Provides buyers with assistance, including financial incentives, to buy a home.	Assistance may include reduced down payments, tax breaks, and lowered requirements for obtaining credit.	Only first-time homebuyers are eligible.
FHA-insured loan: A loan in which the Federal Housing Administration insures the lender against the borrowers' possible default or failure to pay.	Helps lower- and moderate-income people purchase homes. Interest rates may be lower than conventional loans.	Must meet income requirements to be eligible. Home being bought and certain loan terms must meet FHA standards.
VA-guaranteed loan: A long-term, fixed rate mortgage insured by the Veterans Administration for veterans of the U.S. Armed Forces.	No down payment requirements. Interest rates usually are lower than the current market rate.	Only veterans of the U.S. Armed Forces are eligible.

Chapter 19
Transportation

Transportation Choices

Activity A

Chapter 19

Name _______________________________

Date _______________ Period _______________

Describe your transportation needs and the transportation choices available in your community. Name advantages and disadvantages of each form of transportation available. Then answer the question below.

Your transportation needs: (Student response.) ____________________________

____

Available forms of transportation:

1. (Student response.) ____

   Advantages: (Student response.) _______________________________

   Disadvantages: (Student response.) ____________________________

2. (Student response.) ____

   Advantages: (Student response.) _______________________________

   Disadvantages: (Student response.) ____________________________

3. (Student response.) ____

   Advantages: (Student response.) _______________________________

   Disadvantages: (Student response.) ____________________________

4. (Student response.) ____

   Advantages: (Student response.) _______________________________

   Disadvantages: (Student response.) ____________________________

5. (Student response.) ____

   Advantages: (Student response.) _______________________________

   Disadvantages: (Student response.) ____________________________

Which form of transportation best meets your needs? Explain your answer. (Student response.) ____

____

____

____

The Facts and Myths About Car Financing

<table>
<tr><td>Activity B</td><td>Name ___________________________________</td></tr>
<tr><td>Chapter 19</td><td>Date ___________________   Period ______________</td></tr>
</table>

Write true or false in the space provided. Correct any false statements.

__T__   1. Car dealer financing is a convenient, on-the-spot source of financing that may carry a high price tag.

__T__   2. Financing a car costs more than paying cash because you pay interest on the money borrowed.

__F__   3. The minimum age for obtaining a car loan is 16.

__F__   4. When you lease a car, you do not need to pay for registration, licensing, and other charges.

__T__   5. An installment loan is repaid in equal monthly payments over a period of time.

__T__   6. A car with a higher residual value will have lower monthly lease payments.

__T__   7. Lower monthly payments and longer repayment periods increase the amount of interest you pay on a loan.

__T__   8. To obtain auto financing, the borrower must pledge the car as security or collateral.

__F__   9. The higher the rate of interest you are charged, the less money you pay.

__T__   10. The more money you borrow, the more interest you pay.

__T__   11. The longer you borrow money, the more interest you pay.

__T__   12. You can pay less by increasing the size of monthly payments and shortening the repayment period.

__T__   13. The Truth in Lending Law requires creditors to provide borrowers with a complete written account of credit terms and costs.

__F__   14. The capitalized cost of a leased car is the worth of a car at the end of a lease.

__T__   15. Before signing any car loan agreement, be sure to read it carefully.

The "On Paper" Car Review

Activity C

Chapter 19

Name _______________________________

Date _______________ Period _______________

Use the following checklist to evaluate a car you might consider buying for yourself or your family. Summarize your evaluation of the car in the space provided.

	Good	Fair	Poor	Comments
Cost factors				(Chart answers are student response.)
Total price of the car, including options, taxes, delivery charges, preparation charges, and all other fees				
Estimated cost of servicing and maintenance				
Fuel economy				
Warranty coverage				
Number of miles				
Period of time				
Parts covered				
Labor covered				
Responsibilities of the buyer				
Safety features and considerations				
Air bags				
Seat belts				
Visibility				
Anti-lock brakes				
Traction control				
Ease of handling				
Comfort and convenience				
Air conditioning				
Automatic transmission				
Smooth riding				
Sound insulation				
Passenger space				
Seating comfort				
Ease of getting in and out				
Luggage space				

(Continued)

Name _______________________________

	Good	Fair	Poor	Comments
Other options				
Cruise control				
Power windows and locks				
Power seats				
Leather seats				
Sunroof				
Sound system				
Deal and dealer				
Reputation of dealer				
Service facilities				
Availability of parts				
Efficiency of service				
Convenient location				
Appearance of car				
Design				
Model				
Color				
Interior				

My overall impression of this car is _(Student response.)_ ___________________________

____

____

____

____

____

____

____

____

____

Car Operation and Maintenance

Name _______________________________

Date ________________ Period _______________

Discuss the following statements with an automotive technician. Place a check next to each statement that describes proper operation or maintenance of a car.

✓____ 1. Understand the purpose of every gauge and switch on the dashboard and steering column and know how to read or operate each one properly.

_____ 2. If a warning light flashes, wait until it's convenient to investigate the problem.

✓____ 3. Before starting your car, adjust all mirrors so that you can see the traffic behind you and to the side of you.

✓____ 4. For safety, infants and small children should ride in approved safety seats.

✓____ 5. Adults should wear seat belts.

✓____ 6. Try to anticipate stops to avoid unnecessary braking and sudden stops except in emergencies.

_____ 7. It is safe to read maps, sightsee, eat, and drink while driving.

✓____ 8. To avoid being hit from the rear, always signal in advance your intentions to turn, stop, change lanes, or park.

✓____ 9. For routine maintenance, frequently check the fluids that keep brakes, battery, radiator, power steering, and automatic transmission running smoothly.

_____ 10. For safer driving and better fuel economy, keep the tire pressure below the recommended level.

✓____ 11. Whenever your car makes a strange noise, investigate the problem.

✓____ 12. To get reliable auto servicing, look for ASE certified technicians who have completed the training and passed the tests of the National Institute for Automotive Service Excellence.

_____ 13. The best time to shop for auto servicing is when your car will not run.

✓____ 14. Several times a year, check headlights, brake and signal lights, and tire pressure.

✓____ 15. Ask for price estimates before specific services or repairs are performed.

✓____ 16. Read the owner's manual thoroughly and follow the recommended maintenance schedule.

_____ 17. For the best mileage, use high octane gasoline, even in economy cars.

_____ 18. Change the oil and oil filter three times per year.

✓____ 19. Frequent lubrications extend the life of any car.

✓____ 20. Check and replenish windshield washer fluid frequently.

Before Buying a Two-Wheeler

Activity E

Chapter 19

Name _______________________

Date _______________   Period _______________

Find out and describe the licensing, registration, and driving restrictions that apply to bicycles, mopeds, motor scooters, and motorcycles in your area. Check both local and state laws.

Bicycles: (Student response.)

____

____

____

____

Mopeds and motor scooters: (Student response.)

____

____

____

____

Motorcycles: (Student response.)

____

____

____

____

Explain why it is important to consider the information above before buying or operating a two-wheeler.

(Student response.)

____

____

____

____

____

Chapter 20
Electronics and Appliances
Consumer Electronics Inventory

Activity A

Chapter 20

Name ______________________________

Date ___________________   Period ________________

List the appliances and consumer electronics products you and your family use. A few examples of common items are provided for areas of a typical home.

Living room/family room (television, DVD player, gaming system) (Student response.) ______________

____

Bedroom (clock radio, television, music player, air conditioner) (Student response.) ______________

____

Kitchen (refrigerator, microwave, coffeemaker, phone) (Student response.) ______________

____

Bathroom (hair dryer, electric shaver, shower radio) (Student response.) ______________

____

Basement or laundry room (washer, dryer, vacuum cleaner) (Student response.) ______________

____

Outside home, yard, and mobile devices (auto GPS device, cell phone, MP3 player, PDA) ___________
(Student response.)

____

What is the total number of products in your home? (Student response.) ______________

____

____

Computer Knowledge Quiz

<table>
<tr><td>Activity B</td><td>Name _______________________________</td></tr>
<tr><td>Chapter 20</td><td>Date _________________   Period _______________</td></tr>
</table>

Read the statements below concerning computers. Circle *T* if the statement is true or *F* if the statement is false.

T F   1. An operating system controls the basic functions of a computer.

T **F**   2. In general, the faster a computer is, the less it costs.

T **F**   3. An anti-virus program kills germs on a computer keyboard and mouse.

T F   4. Programs that help users prepare spreadsheets and presentations are examples of application software.

T F   5. Its microprocessor and RAM determine a computer's processing speed.

T **F**   6. Laptops generally offer more capabilities for less money than desktops.

T F   7. Cell phones and other handheld devices can use computer programs.

T **F**   8. Peripheral devices include computer software and the operating system.

T **F**   9. A firewall protects your computer from explosions and accidental fire.

T F   10. Phishing is the act of sending official-looking messages to trick computer users into revealing their financial and identity information.

T **F**   11. *Wi-Fi* is short for *Wireless Finances*.

T F   12. A USB port is where peripheral devices can be plugged into a computer.

T **F**   13. A hotspot is the only place in a person's home where a laptop computer can connect to the Internet.

T **F**   14. A kilobit is the smallest unit of data a computer uses.

T F   15. As bandwidth increases, so does the amount of information that can be carried over an electronic cable or device at one time.

Is This a Good Deal?

Name ______________________________

Date ________________   Period ________________

Free phone with 2-year agreement and unlimited messaging plan*!

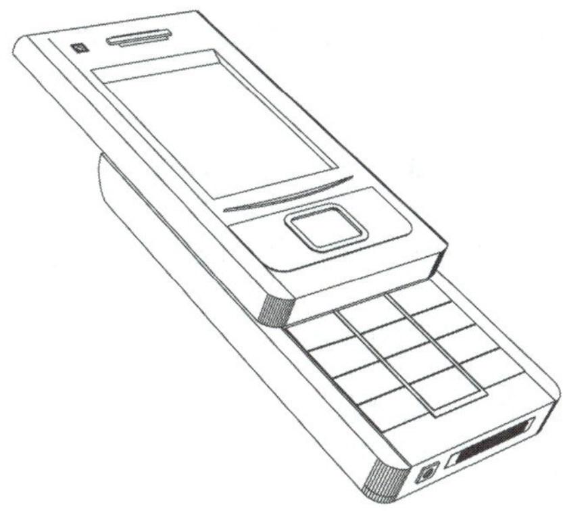

Package includes:

Super Cell Phone—$200 value **FREE!**

1. Choose one of the following phone service plans:
   - Unlimited Minutes $100/month
   - 1200 Minutes $80/month
   - 900 Minutes $60/month
   - 425 Minutes $40/month
2. Choose one of the following plans:
   - Unlimited messaging and data $35/month
   - Unlimited messaging only $25/month

*2-year contract required. $200 activation fee will appear on your first bill.

1. What is the minimum amount you would pay in fees over the life of the contract? (Do not include taxes, insurance, overages, and other fees.) $65 minimum/month or $1,560 over two years (24 months) + $200 activation fee = $1,760

2. What is the maximum amount you would pay in fees over the life of the contract? (Do not include taxes, insurance, overages, and other fees.) $135 maximum/month or $3,240 over two years + $200 activation fee = $3,440

3. Under what circumstances is this offer a good deal? It is a good deal if you talk much more than 425 minutes a month and heavily use messaging and data features. Otherwise, a pay-as-you-go plan and buying a cheaper phone would be better.

Calculating Energy Use

Name _______________________________

Date _________________   Period _______________

Energy use is measured in watts. A kilowatt is equal to 1,000 watts. The maximum wattage used by an electronic product or small appliance is given on its label or nameplate. You can use this figure to calculate the product's estimated energy use and annual cost of operation. The following formulas help you do this. They are provided on the U.S. Department of Energy's Web site (www.energysavers.gov/your_home/appliances):

- Wattage × Hours used per day ÷ 1,000 = Energy used per day in kilowatts per hour, or kWh

- Energy used per day × Number of days per year the item is operating = Energy used per year

- Energy used per year × Your electricity rate per kWh = Annual operating cost

Calculate the annual cost of using each of the following, assuming that each product is used 4 hours a day, 200 days a year. Also assume that your electricity rate is 5.4 cents (or .054 dollars) per kWh. Show your work.

A. Clothes dryer (4,000 Watts) _16 kWh per day; 3,200 kWh per year; $172.80 per year_

B. Personal laptop computer (50 Watts) _.02 kWh per day; 40 kWh per year; $2.16 per year_

C. Flat-screen television (120 Watts) _.48 kWh per day; 96 kWh per year; $5.18 per year_

Shopping for Major Home Appliances

Activity E

Chapter 20

Name ______________________________

Date ________________ Period ______________

Shop for a major home appliance. Fill in information about the appliance in the space below.

Appliance: _(Student response.)_____________________________

Selling price: _(Student response.)_____________________________

Charges: Delivery _(Student response.)___ Installation _(Student response.)___

Credit _(Student response.)___ Other _(Student response.)___

Projected operating costs or energy efficiency rating: _(Student response.)_____________

Safety features: _(Student response.)_____________________________

____

____

Performance features: _(Student response.)_____________________________

____

____

Economy features: _(Student response.)_____________________________

____

____

Warranty provisions: _(Student response.)_____________________________

____

____

Facilities and provisions for servicing: _(Student response.)_____________

____

Space requirements: _(Student response.)_____________________________

Power requirements: _(Student response.)_____________________________

Ease of use, care, and maintenance: _(Student response.)_____________

____

Reliability and reputation of dealer/seller: _(Student response.)___________

Reliability and reputation of manufacturer: _(Student response.)___________

Comments: _(Student response.)_____________________________

____

____

Prioritizing Job Attributes

Activity A

Chapter 21

Name _______________________________

Date _________________   Period _______________

You can begin to think now about what you want in an ideal job or career. In what type of environment do you wish to work? What aspects of a job are most important to you? Following is a list of job characteristics and values. Rate each a *1*, *2*, or *3* depending on how important it is to you.

(Ratings are student response.)

1 most important

2 of medium importance

3 least important

_______ Working independently from others

_______ Working closely with other people

_______ Earning a high salary

_______ Having a prestigious job title

_______ Doing something I enjoy

_______ Having good benefits

_______ Having flexible work hours

_______ Having a manageable workload

_______ Being able to work from home

_______ Working with people I like

_______ Feeling secure in my job

_______ Knowing what to expect each day

_______ Not knowing what to expect each day

_______ Juggling a variety of tasks

_______ Working in a fast-paced environment

_______ Working in a low-stress environment

_______ Working for a prestigious company

_______ Having a comfortable office or job site

_______ Doing a lot of traveling on the job

_______ Having the latest technology at my disposal

_______ Having a short commute

_______ Working for a company with family-friendly policies

_______ Having many opportunities for advancement

In the spaces below, write the job attributes you rated most important. Then rank those attributes in order of their importance to you. Keep these preferences in mind as you think about possible careers. Your preferences may change as you grow older.

(Student response.)

____

____

____

____

____

Making a Career Plan

Name _______________________________

Date _________________ Period _______________

Choose an occupation in which you are interested. Write the occupation on the blank line below. Using the *Occupational Outlook Handbook* and other career resources, create a career plan like the one in Figure 21-5 for the occupation you have chosen.

Career Plan for _______________________________			
	Education and Training	**Work Experience**	**Personal Projects and Activities**
Junior High School	(Chart answers are student response.)		
Senior High School			
College			
After College			

Choosing a College

<table>
<tr><td>Activity C</td><td>Name ___________________________</td></tr>
<tr><td>Chapter 21</td><td>Date _____________ Period _____________</td></tr>
</table>

If you are considering college, complete the following form for each school you are interested in attending.

Name of school _(Answers are student response.)_____________________

Address ____

City____________________________ State ___________________

Zip_________________________ Telephone ___________________

Accreditation____

Number of students________ Male________ Female________

Class sizes________ Student/faculty ratio________

Program and course offerings, particularly in your area of interest: ______________
____

Reputation and standing, especially in your field of interest: ___________________
____

Facilities for student use (academic, computer, athletic, social): _______________
____

The campus environment (living facilities, campus size and setting, extracurricular activities):
____
____

Financial aid opportunities and job availability:_____________________________

Estimated Costs: **Admission Requirements:**

Estimated Costs		Admission Requirements	
Tuition	$ ________	Grade point average	________
Room and board	________	Class rank	________
Fees	________	SAT scores	________
Books and supplies	________	ACT scores	________
Transportation	________	Interview	________
Miscellaneous	________	Other	________
Total	$ ________		

Comments: _(Student response.)_________________________________
____

Choosing an Occupational Training Program

Activity D

Chapter 21

Name _______________________________

Date _________________ Period _______________

If you expect to enter an occupational training program, complete the following form to evaluate a program you are considering.

Name of school (Answers are student response.) _______________________________

Program description _______________________________

Address_______________________________ City_______________ State_________

Zip_______________ Telephone _______________________________

Certification or degree conferred: _______________________________

Courses or training offered/skills to be mastered:_______________________________

____

____

____

Number of hours per week: _________ Length of time to completion: _______________

Qualifications and reputation of instructors: _______________________________

____

Requirements for enrollment: _______________________________

____

Adequacy of facilities, equipment, and supplies for student use:_______________________________

____

Job outlook and placement record for graduates: _______________________________

____

Estimated Costs: Tuition $ _____________

Books   _____________

Equipment
and supplies   _____________

Fees   _____________

Room/board   _____________

Other   _____________

Total $ _____________

Comments:_______________________________

____

____

Activity A   Name _______________________________________

Chapter 22   Date ________________   Period _______________

Complete the following sample job application form.

APPLICATION FOR EMPLOYMENT

PERSONAL INFORMATION   (All information is student response.)

Date ____

Name ____

       Last   First   Middle

Present Address ______________________________

       Street   City   State   Zip

Permanent Address ___________________________

       Street   City   State   Zip

Phone Number ________________________________

If related to anyone in our employ,   Referred

state name and department   by ________________

EMPLOYMENT DESIRED

Position ________   Date you can start ________   Salary desired ________

Are you employed now? ________   If so, may we inquire of your present employer? ________

Ever applied to this company before? ________   Where ________   When ________

EDUCATION

	Name and Location of School	Years Completed	Subjects Studied
Grammar School			
High School			
College			
Trade, Business, or Correspondence School			

Subject of special study or research work _______________________________________

____

(Continued)

Name ____

U.S. Military or Naval service	Rank		Present membership in National Guard or Reserves

Activities other than religious (civic, athletic, fraternal, etc.)

____

Exclude organizations the name or character of which indicates the race, creed, color, or national origin of its members

____

FORMER EMPLOYERS   List below last three employers starting with last one first

Date Month and Year	Name and Address of Employer	Salary	Position	Reason for Leaving
From				
To				
From				
To				
From				
To				

REFERENCES   Give below the names of two persons not related to you, whom you have known at least one year

	Name	Address	Job Title	Years Acquainted
1.				
2.				

PHYSICAL RECORD

In case of emergency notify ____

	Name	Address	Phone No.

I authorize investigation of all statements contained in this application. I understand that misrepresentation or omission of facts called for is cause for dismissal.

Date _______________   Signature _______________

Code of Workplace Ethics

Name ______________________________

Date ________________   Period ____________

1. Define *ethics* and *workplace ethics*. *Ethics* are a set of moral values that guide a person's behavior. *Workplace ethics* generally address relationships of the business with employees, customers, suppliers, investors, creditors, competitors, and community.

2. Explain briefly why ethics is important in the workplace for
   - employers fair treatment of employees, teamwork, competition, conflicts of interest
   - employees workplace relationships, use of business resources and assets, confidentiality
   - clients and customers confidentiality, competition, and conflicts of interest
   - the business community environmental concerns, use of business resources and assets

3. Write at least one example of ethical behavior in connection with each of the following:
   - Work ethic (Student response.)

   - Coworkers (Student response.)

   - Employers (Student response.)

   - Use of work facilities, supplies, and equipment (Student response.)

   - Customers (Student response.)

   - Business or organization loyalty (Student response.)

   - Confidentiality (Student response.)

   - Honesty (Student response.)

   - Truthfulness (Student response.)

   - Reliability (Student response.)

   - Workplace gossip (Student response.)

   - Teamwork (Student response.)

Entrepreneurship

Name _______________________________________

Date ___________________   Period _______________

Complete the following exercise to help you decide whether you want to accept the challenge of being an entrepreneur.

1. Does being an entrepreneur appeal to you? _______________ Give three reasons for your answer.
   (Student response.) ____

   ____

   ____

2. Describe a product or service you could sell. (Student response.) ___________________

   ____

3. Briefly describe the market in your area for the item listed above. (Consider potential customers, the need for your product or service, competition, and your sales ability.) (Student response.) ______

   ____

   ____

   ____

4. What expenses would be involved in getting started and continuing to operate your business? (Expense items may include space, facilities, equipment, supplies, payroll, advertising, transportation, insurance, taxes, etc.) Prepare a list of expenses and estimate the costs.

Expenses	Estimated Costs
(Student response.)	(Student response.)
	TOTAL _______________

5. Based on your answers to the above questions, what are at least five pros and five cons of starting a business of your own?

Pros	Cons
(Student response.)	(Student response.)
	TOTAL _______________

6. What government regulations and tax considerations will affect your business? _______________
   (Student response.)

   ____

Making the Most of Your Resources

Activity D   Name _______________________________

Chapter 22   Date _________________ Period _____________

Use the following worksheet to evaluate your available resources and plan ways to use them.

Resources	
Category	**Description**
Time: List how much free time you have each day and at what time of the day.	(Student response.)
Money: List amounts available in savings or from a job or an allowance.	(Student response.)
Abilities and talents: List anything you do well.	(Student response.)
Experience: Outline what you have done and can do because of the experience.	(Student response.)
Tools and equipment: Include any item available for you to use, such as a computer, sewing machine, or car.	(Student response.)
Other:	(Student response.)

Study your list of resources. Think of at least three ways you could put your resources to work for economic gain. Describe your ideas below.

1. (Student response.)

2. (Student response.)

3. (Student response.)

(Continued)

Name ____

Select one of the ideas you listed and create a plan outlining the steps you would take in carrying out your idea.

Describe your business or project: _(Student response.)_________________________________

____

Write down the steps necessary to carry out your idea in the order they should be done.

1. _(Steps are student response.)____

2. ____

3. ____

4. ____

5. ____

List the materials and space you would need. Then estimate the cost of each.

Materials and Space	**Estimated Cost**
(Student response.)	(Student response.)

Describe the advertising and publicity you would use to attract buyers.

(Student response.)____

____

____

Answer the following questions.

1. What goods or services would you offer? (Student response.)_______________________

2. Who would be your customers? (Student response.)_______________________________

3. Who would be your competition? (Student response.)______________________________

4. How much would you expect to sell? (Student response.)__________________________

5. What would be your cost of providing the goods or services? (Student response.)_______

6. What would you charge? (Student response.)___________________________________

7. What would be your profit? (Student response.)_________________________________

Chapter 23
Your Role in the Environment

Reality Check

Name _________________________________

Date _________________ Period _________________

How much are you really doing for the environment? Check all that apply.
(Answers are student response.)

_______ 1. I keep myself informed about local environmental issues.

_______ 2. I realize that small acts, such as tossing one wrapper out of the car window, can lead to big environmental problems.

_______ 3. I avoid wasting water, food, gas, and electricity.

_______ 4. I recycle newspapers, magazines, glass, and plastics.

_______ 5. I make an effort to reduce noise pollution.

_______ 6. I participate in community projects that enhance and protect the environment.

_______ 7. I avoid unnecessary and careless use of pesticides and harsh chemicals.

_______ 8. When shopping, I look for products that can be recycled and avoid overpackaged products.

_______ 9. I support candidates who take stands on environmental issues.

_______ 10. I respect natural resources as economic assets.

_______ 11. My home is well-insulated to conserve energy.

_______ 12. I turn off electrical equipment when not in use.

_______ 13. I avoid running water unnecessarily, such as when I brush my teeth.

_______ 14. I avoid using dishwashers, clothes washers, and dryers during peak energy usage times.

_______ 15. I walk or bike when possible.

_______ 16. I carpool when possible.

_______ 17. I follow fuel-conserving driving practices.

_______ 18. I take care to repair leaky faucets promptly.

_______ 19. When buying appliances, I look for energy- and water-saving features.

_______ 20. I conserve water used in the yard by watering in the early morning or evening.

Count the number of statements you checked. Do you consider yourself a friend to the environment?
Why or why not? (Student response.) ____

____

____

It's on the Meter

Name _______________________________

Date _________________   Period _______________

Read the instructions on how to read electric and gas meters. Then read and record the following meter settings. The first reading is done for you.

Electric meters measure usage in kilowatt-hours (kWh). Gas meters measure usage in cubic feet.

Meters usually have four or five dials. Always start to read your meter with the first dial on the right. Note that some of dials run clockwise, while others run counterclockwise.

If the pointer is between numbers, write the smaller number. However, if the pointer is between zero and 9, write 9.

If a pointer is directly on a number, look at the dial to the right. If the pointer is anywhere between zero and 5, write the number directly under the pointer in question. If the pointer is between 6 and 9, write the smaller number.

1. 

8

4

2

4

2. 

7

9

1

1

3. 

9

5

7

5

4. 

7

2

4

1

5. 

8

1

7

7

Energy Conservation

Name ____

Date ____________________ Period __________________

In each column below, list nine ways that you and your family can conserve energy. Place a star next to the things you do routinely. Underline those that you have not done in the past, but would be willing to do.

Energy Savers

In the home:	On the road:
1. (Chart answers are student response.)	1.
2.	2.
3.	3.
4.	4.
5.	5.
6.	6.
7.	7.
8.	8.
9.	9.

Action You Can Take

Name ___________________________

Date _______________ Period _______________

List an action that you would be willing to take to curb pollution and protect the environment in each of the following areas:

1. Solid waste disposal: (Student response.) ___________________________

____

____

2. Noise pollution: (Student response.) ___________________________

____

____

3. Air pollution: (Student response.) ___________________________

____

____

4. Water pollution: (Student response.) ___________________________

____

____

5. Nuclear waste disposal: (Student response.) ___________________________

____

____

6. Conservation of natural resources: (Student response.) ___________________________

____

____

7. Preservation of forests and wetlands: (Student response.) ___________________________

____

____

8. Population control: (Student response.) ___________________________

____

____

9. Beautification in your area: (Student response.) ___________________________

____

____

10. Urban sprawl: (Student response.) ___________________________

____

____

Where Has All the Gasoline Gone?

Name ________________________________

Date ________________   Period ________________

Read the scenario and answer the discussion questions.

Suppose our nation is facing a severe fuel shortage. Lines at service stations are two and three blocks long. Most stations close on weekends, and many run out of gasoline by Thursday afternoon. Supplies that are available are sold on a first-come, first-served basis. This creates problems for all the people who must drive to work. In many areas, the public transit system is neither adequate nor reliable enough to replace private cars.

Listed below are some possible alternatives for dealing with this situation.

   a. Strictly enforce a 55 miles per hour speed limit.

   b. Raise the price of gasoline to lower demand. At the same time, develop a gas stamp program to aid the needy and those who must drive to work.

   c. Allocate more funds for further development of synthetic fuels.

   d. Improve relations with countries that export petroleum and make whatever agreements are necessary to get more fuel.

   e. Raise the driving age.

   f. Close shopping centers, service stations, and other facilities on Sundays to reduce unnecessary driving.

   g. Penalize families that own more than one car.

   h. Increase costs connected with driving and car ownership, such as licenses, parking fees, and permits.

   i. Reward carpooling by requiring all single passenger auto commuters to buy special permits.

   j. Place a heavy tax on automobiles that do not meet high fuel economy standards.

   k. Restrict the sale of private cars and require auto owner permits based on transportation needs.

   l. Allocate more funds to develop fuel-efficient public transportation.

   1. Consider the costs, benefits, and consequences of each alternative. What choices would you make? Which do you think would be most effective? (Student response.)

   ____

   ____

   ____

   ____

   ____

(Continued)

Name _______________________________________

2. Which alternatives would be the most costly for government? _______________________________
   (Answers may vary.) a, b, c, d, l

   ____

3. Which alternatives would be the most costly for consumers? (Answers may vary.) b, g, h, i, j, k

   ____

4. Which alternatives would be the most inconvenient? (Answers may vary.) d, e, f, i, k

   ____

5. What other possible alternatives can you suggest? (Student response.)

   ____

   ____

   ____

   ____

   ____

   ____

   ____

6. Which alternatives would affect you personally? Explain. (Student response.)

   ____

   ____

   ____

   ____

   ____

   ____

   ____

   ____